Multilateral In

Multilateral Institutions

A Critical Introduction

Morten Bøås and Desmond McNeill

Pluto Press

LONDON • STERLING, VIRGINIA

First published 2003 by Pluto Press
345 Archway Road, London N6 5AA
and 22883 Quicksilver Drive,
Sterling, VA 20166–2012, USA

www.plutobooks.com

British Library Cataloguing in Publication Data
A catalogue record for this book is available from the British Library

ISBN 0 7453 1921 1 hardback
ISBN 0 7453 1920 3 paperback

Library of Congress Cataloging in Publication Data
Bøås, Morten, 1965-
    Multilateral institutions : a critical introduction / Morten Bøås and
Desmond McNeill.
        p. cm.
Includes bibliographical references and index.
    ISBN 0–7453–1921–1 (hbk) — ISBN 0–7453–1920–3 (pbk.)
    1. Financial institutions, International. 2. International agencies.
3. Non–governmental organizations. 4. Globalization. 5. Sovereignty.
6. Economic assistance. 7. World Bank. 8. International Monetary
Fund. 9. World Trade Organization. I. McNeill, Desmond. II. Title.
    HG3881 .B556 2003
    341.7'5'06—dc21
                                                            2002015929

10   9   8   7   6   5   4   3   2   1

Designed and produced for Pluto Press by
Chase Publishing Services, Fortescue, Sidmouth, England
Typeset from disk by Stanford DTP Services, Towcester, England
Printed and bound in the European Union by
Antony Rowe, Chippenham and Eastbourne, England

Contents

List of Tables

Acknowledgements

This book is one of the products of a collaboration between a political scientist (Morten Bøås) and an economist (Desmond McNeill) who, on the basis of very different experience, and for rather different reasons, found a common theoretical interest in, and practical commitment to, the topic of multilateral institutions in development. We woud like to thank the Research Council of Norway, and more specifically the programme entitled 'The multilateral system in the field of develoment', which has provided generous financial support for our research. The programme also organised annual conferences at which research in progress was discussed. At the last of these, in Bergen in May 2002, an outline of the book was presented, and we are grateful for valuable comments received on that occasion. We would like to thank Anne Engh for valuable assistance in the preparation of this book. Our research has involved contacts with several multilateral organisations, and we are grateful for assistance from staff of the Royal Norwegian Ministry of Foreign Affairs – Ingrid Glad, Paal Aavatsmark, Olav Seim, Trond Folke Lindberg and others – in this regard, without in any way attributing to them responsibility for our findings. At Pluto Press we are grateful to Roger van Zwanenberg, Julie Stoll and Robert Webb for their efficiency and support, and, for her copy-editing, Jeanne Brady. Last, and certainly not least, we thank the Centre for Development and the Environment (SUM) at the University of Oslo, for hosting the project, and providing a most stimulating and supportive milieu throughout.

Abbreviations

ABCDE	Annual Bank Conference on Development Economics
ADB	Asian Development Bank
ADF	African Development Fund
AfDB	African Development Bank
ASEAN	Association of South East Asian Nations
ATTAC	Association pour une Taxation des Transactions Financières L'aide aux Citoyens
CIEL	Center for International Environmental Law
CTE	Committee on Trade and Environment
EBRD	European Bank for Reconstruction and Development
ECOSOC	United Nations Economic and Social Council
ED	executive director
EDF	Environmental Defence Fund
EF	Environmental Defence
EFTA	European Free Trade Area
EIB	European Investment Bank
EMIT	Working Group on Environmental Measures and International Trade
EPI	Environmental Policy Institute
FoE	Friends of the Earth
GATT	General Agreement on Tariffs and Trade
GAVI	Global Alliance for Vaccination and Immunisation
GCI	general capital increase
GDP	gross domestic product
GEF	Global Environment Facility
GMS	Greater Mekong Subregion
GNP	gross national product
HDR	*Human Development Report*
IBRD	International Bank for Reconstruction and Development
ICOLD	International Commission on Large Dams
IDA	International Development Association
IDB	Inter-American Development Bank
IFC	International Finance Corporation
ILO	International Labour Organisation
IMF	International Monetary Fund

IRN	International Rivers Network
JBIC	Japan Bank for International Co-operation
JEXIM	Export–Import Bank of Japan
MDB	Multilateral development bank
NGO	Non-governmental organisation
NRDC	National Resources Defence Council
NWF	National Wildlife Federation
ODA	official development assistance
OECD	Organisation for Economic Cooperation and Development
RDB	regional development banks
SAP	structural adjustment programme
SRF	supplementary reserve facility
SUNFED	Special UN Fund for Economic Development
TA	technical assistance
UN	United Nations
UNCED	United Nations Conference on Environment and Development
UNCHE	United Nations Conference on the Human Environment
UNCTAD	United Nations Conference on Trade and Development
UNDP	United Nations Development Programme
UNECA	United Nations Economic Commission for Africa
UNF	United Nations Foundation
UNFIP	United Nations Fund for International Partnerships
UNHCR	United Nations High Commission for Refugees
USAID	United States Agency for International Development Aid
WCED	World Commission on Environment and Development
WDR	*World Development Report*
WTO	World Trade Organisation
WWF	World Wildlife Fund

Multilateral Institutions: A Brief Guide[1]

WORLD BANK

Main activity: The World Bank provides long-term loans to governments for development projects, and short-term loans (1–3 years) for institutional policy reforms. The World Bank also provides technical assistance, mainly in the form of advice to governments in borrowing countries.[2]

Headquarters: Washington, DC, USA

Geographical area: Global: Middle-income countries (countries with per capita incomes between US$1506 and US$5445) and poorer countries defined as 'creditworthy' borrow from the International Bank for Reconstruction and Development (IBRD), while the poorest countries (with per capita incomes of less than US$885) borrow from the International Development Association (IDA). Loans granted by the IDA are interest-free but borrowers pay a service charge of less than 1 per cent of the loan to cover administrative costs.

Country offices: 97

Staff: Approximately 10,000, of whom 8,000+ are based in Washington, DC

Financial disbursements (in 2001): Total: US$17,251 million (60.79 per cent in hard loans and 39.20 per cent in soft loans)

Credit rating: AAA

Ownership structure: 184 member countries.

Voting Power in the IBRD

Selected countries[3]	Per cent of total
United States	16.40
Japan	7.87
Germany	4.49
France	4.31
United Kingdom	4.31
China	2.79
India	2.79
Indonesia	0.94

Brazil	2.07
Argentina	1.12
Mexico	1.18
Nigeria	0.80
South Africa	0.85
Egypt	0.45

INTERNATIONAL MONETARY FUND

Main activity: The International Monetary Fund (IMF) lends money to member countries facing balance-of-payments problems. In return for financial assistance from the IMF, borrowing countries must implement economic reforms. Loans are disbursed in instalments and payment is tied to compliance with structural adjustment targets. The IMF also provides technical assistance in the form of: (a) design and implementation of fiscal and monetary policies, (b) institution building (for example, central bank, treasury, tax and customs departments, and statistical services), and (c) drafting and review of economic and financial legislation.
Headquarters: Washington, DC, USA
Geographical area: Global
Country offices: None
Staff: 2650
Financial (positive) commitments (in 2001): Total: US$18,154 million (91.29 per cent in hard loans and 8.70 per cent in soft loans)
Credit rating: Not applicable
Ownership structure: 184 member countries

Voting Power

Selected countries	Per cent of total
United States	17.11
Japan	6.14
Germany	6.00
France	4.95
United Kingdom	4.95
China	2.94
India	1.93
Indonesia	0.97
Brazil	1.41
Argentina	0.99
Mexico	1.20

Nigeria	0.82
South Africa	0.87
Egypt	0.45

ASIAN DEVELOPMENT BANK

Main activity: The Asian Development Bank (ADB) extends loans, equity investments and technical assistance to its regional developing member countries.
Headquarters: Manila, Philippines
Geographical area: Asia and the Pacific
Country offices: 15
Staff: 2163
Financial disbursements (in 2001): Total: US$3,874 million (73.56 per cent in hard loans and 26.44 per cent in soft loans)
Credit rating: AAA
Ownership structure: 61 member countries, of whom 44 are from the region

Voting Power

Selected countries	Per cent of total
United States	13.05
Japan	13.05
Germany	2.86
France	2.24
United Kingdom	2.00
China	5.59
India	5.48
Indonesia	4.78
Brazil	—
Argentina	—
Mexico	—
Nigeria	—
South Africa	—
Egypt	—

INTER-AMERICAN DEVELOPMENT BANK

Main activity: The Inter-American Development Bank (IDB) provides loans and technical assistance to its regional developing member countries.

Headquarters: Washington, DC, USA
Geographical area: Latin America and the Caribbean
Country offices: 26
Staff: 1730 of whom 526 are attached to country offices
Financial disbursements (in 2001): Total: US$6,459 million (93.46 per cent in hard loans and 6.53 per cent in soft loans)
Credit rating: AAA
Ownership structure: 46 member countries of whom 26 are from the region

Voting Power

Selected countries	Per cent of total
United States	30.01
Japan	5.00
Germany	1.90
France	1.90
United Kingdom	0.96
China	—
India	—
Indonesia	—
Brazil	10.75
Argentina	10.75
Mexico	6.91
Nigeria	—
South Africa	—
Egypt	—

AFRICAN DEVELOPMENT BANK

Main activity: The African Development Bank (AfDB) provides loans and technical assistance to its regional member countries.
Headquarters: Abidjan, Côte d'Ivoire
Geographical area: Africa
Country offices: 4
Staff: 1026 of whom 917 are from regional member countries
Financial disbursements (in 2001): Total: U.$1,076 million (56.64 per cent in hard loans and 43.36 per cent in soft loans)
Credit rating: AA+
Ownership structure: 77 member countries of whom 53 are from the region

Voting Power

Selected countries	Per cent of total
United States	6.57
Japan	5.42
Germany	4.09
France	3.72
United Kingdom	1.68
China	1.13
India	0.25
Indonesia	—
Brazil	0.47
Argentina	0.32
Mexico	—
Nigeria	8.87
South Africa	3.97
Egypt	5.12

WORLD TRADE ORGANISATION

Main activity: The World Trade Organisation (WTO) constitutes the global forum for trade negotiations and for handling trade disputes. It administers the GATT/WTO trade agreements, monitors national trade policies, and provides technical assistance to developing countries.

Headquarters: Geneva, Switzerland

Geographical area: Global

Country offices: None

Staff: 560 of whom 94 are from developing member countries

Financial disbursements: None

Credit rating: Not applicable

Ownership structure: 144 member countries (30 of which are least-developed countries according to the UN's classification). The principle for decision making is 'one country, one vote', but decisions are almost always by consensus. An integral part of WTO's decision-making structure is the Dispute Settlement Mechanism.

UNITED NATIONS DEVELOPMENT PROGRAMME

Main activity: The United Nations Development Programme (UNDP) provides developing countries with technical assistance in order to assist them in attracting and using aid effectively to alleviate poverty.

Headquarters: New York, USA (and in addition headquarter offices in Washington, DC, London, Copenhagen, Brussels, Geneva, Rome, Tokyo, Oslo and Stockholm)

Geographical area: Global (currently involved in 166 countries)

Country offices: 122

Staff: 4,000 of whom approximately 1,000 staff members work at the nine headquarter offices outside New York

Credit rating: Not applicable

Budget resources – net core and donor co-financing (in 2001): Total: US$ 1,300 million

Ownership structure: All 189 UN member countries are eligible for membership. The Executive Board of UNDP is formally placed under the authority of the UN's Economic and Social Council (ECOSOC). ECOSOC elects a new Executive Board annually. The Executive Board is comprised of 36 members based on the following geographical distribution of members: Africa (8), Asia and the Pacific (7), Eastern Europe (4), Latin America and the Caribbean (5) and Western Europe and North America (12).

Top 10 contributors to UNDP's core resources (2001)

Donors	Net core resources (in US$ millions)
Japan	96.00
United States	79.24
Norway	68.82
Netherlands	66.28
Sweden	53.08
United Kingdom	52.91
Denmark	49.29
Switzerland	29.21
Canada	26.94
Belgium	22.26

Notes
1. This brief guide draws on information from the following sources: ADB (2002a), AfDB (2002), IDB (2002), IMF (2002a), Standard & Poor's (2001), UNDP (2002), World Bank (2002) and WTO (2002), and information from the websites of these institutions (see the list of internet resources in this book). All data compiled are

from mid-2002. We appreciate the assistance of Erik Blytt in calculating the IMF's Special Drawing Right (SDR) into US dollars.

2. In addition to the IBRD and the IDA, the World Bank *Group* includes the International Finance Corportion (IFC), the Multilateral Investment Guarantee Agency (MIGA) and the International Centre for Settlement of Investment Disputes (ICSID).

3. The five largest donors, plus selected developing countries (three per region).

1
Introduction: A 'Critical Engagement' Approach to Multilateral Institutions

In 1944, as the Second World War neared its end, a conference was convened by the victorious countries in Bretton Woods, in the United States. It was here that the World Bank and the International Monetary Fund were born – in the hope that they would provide the foundations of a peaceful and prosperous future for the world. Fifty years later, these two multilateral institutions occupy a dominant position in the global political economy, but they are the target of powerful attack – both in the streets and in the media. And in the course of these 50 years, they have been joined by a whole range of other multilateral institutions. In the late 1950s and early 1960s, three important regional development banks were established in Latin America, Asia and Africa. In 1965, the United Nations Development Programme was created, supplementing a number of United Nations (UN) specialised agencies some of which had already existed for decades. And in 1995, the World Trade Organisation (WTO) replaced the General Agreement on Tariffs and Trade (GATT), which had been the major framework for global trade negotiations since 1948. This constituted the last of the four pillars of the international system: the International Monetary Fund (IMF), the World Bank, the UN and the WTO – which had originally been conceived at Bretton Woods.

In the course of this period, a great deal had changed. The anniversary of the World Bank and IMF was met with a 'Fifty years is enough' campaign. And the meeting of the WTO in Seattle led to violent clashes in the street, to be followed by the formation of a loosely knit confederation of non-governmental organisations (NGOs) and activists who demonstrated against 'globalisation' in general, and its institutional manifestation (the World Bank, the IMF and the WTO) in particular. While some people see these institutions, and the multilateralism they promote, as playing an important role in the elimination of world poverty, others see them not as the solution, but as part of the problem. There has

1

thus, in recent years, been greatly increased public attention and criticism of the multilateral institutions. Their annual meetings, formerly of little interest to the general public, are now events that hit the headlines of major newspapers all over the world. Many civil society activists view these institutions as part of an undesirable strengthening of market-led globalisation. Mass protest has been organised around World Bank, IMF and WTO meetings, often ending in violent clashes between protesters and huge police forces called out to prevent demonstrators from disturbing the proceedings. The importance of these annual meetings as rallying points for an emerging global anti-globalisation movement, represented by civil society movements such as Association pour une Taxation des Transactions Financièrs pour L'aide aux Citoyens (ATTAC), should not be underestimated.

Entering the new millennium, therefore, the future direction of the multilateral system is one of the most important subjects of public debate. Regrettably, however, this debate is often ill-informed. The views of those who support these institutions and those who argue for their substantial reform or closure are often not based on a well-grounded understanding of the multilateral institutions: how they are financed and organised, and how they interact with client countries, donor countries and each other. This contributes to the failure of effective dialogue between the differing camps. This book is a modest attempt to improve the situation.

This book thus offers students, practitioners and activists a critical introduction to the major institutions that constitute the multilateral development system. The mandate of these institutions defines them as technical and functional organisations. However, we regard them as political organisations whose projects, programmes and policies have a significant impact on domestic policies in the many countries in which they are involved. We will here describe the major institutions that make up the multilateral development financing system: how they operate with respect to financing and lending, and how they are organised. We will assess the various roles that they play, and related changes in their policy concerns, such as structural adjustment, sustainable development, and – more recently – governance. This discussion will be linked to the dominant role played by economics, and how the favoured approach changed over time from a Keynesian one to a neoliberal one. The major multilateral development banks (MDBs) – the

World Bank, the three largest regional development banks, the African Development Bank (AfDB), the Asian Development Bank (ADB) and the Inter-American Development Bank (IDB), and the United Nations Development Programme (UNDP) – will be our main concerns, but we will also discuss the role of the IMF and the WTO *vis-à-vis* these institutions, and the processes and debates around them. These institutions constitute our main reference points, but we do not devote the same attention to each of them. Our main purpose is to facilitate understanding of politics and processes. For instance, in Chapter 4 when we write about the ADB, it is not only because the ADB is important (it is), but also because the political processes in this institution highlight issues of concern also for the larger universe of multilateral institutions.

Another feature of this book which may surprise some readers is the emphasis on NGOs and environmental issues. The reason for this is, however, clear. Over the two last decades NGO interaction with multilateral institutions (both directly and through member states) has been perhaps the single most important cause of reform. This NGO activity is clearly related to environmental issues. Or to phrase our argument in a different manner: it was environmental issues that first offered NGOs and civil society organisations a possibility to access and influence decision-making processes in multilateral institutions. The environment was the first rallying point for NGO activity in the World Bank and later in the regional development banks, the WTO and other multilateral institutions. This is the reason why we devote substantial attention to this particular issue-area of politics in multilateral institutions.

Our emphasis is therefore on politics within and between multilateral institutions. We argue that it is not fruitful to treat multilateral institutions as unitary actors. Just as it is widely recognised in contemporary debate that it is a gross simplification to define the nation-state as a unitary actor, the same should apply to multilateral institutions. Rather than treating each one, such as the World Bank, as a 'black box' we will highlight its internal processes and politics. This discussion will be supplemented by an analysis of the relationships between multilateral institutions, which are both competitive and collaborative. In addition, both member states and NGOs play an important role, as will be demonstrated by reference to a number of examples of the making and testing of policy in practice. The most important of these cases, which marks the emergence of NGOs as a major force in international relations, relates to the Pelosi Amendment in the United States. Other cases we shall refer to include specific projects such as the Arun III Hydro-power project in Nepal and the Samut Prakarn Wastewater Management project in Thailand. These cases will illustrate the complex interplay between member states, multilateral institutions and NGOs in the making of policy.

The approach in this book is critical in the sense that we do not accept the policies and approaches of multilateral institutions at face value, but ask how and why these policies came into existence. However, our criticism is also matched by an argument for engagement. The normative basis of this book is our view that it is important to engage in critical dialogue, both with the member states of multilateral institutions and the institutions themselves, from an independent and informed position. We see a strong need for increased critical engagement – both by researchers and social activists – in order to bring about much needed reform of the approaches and policies of multilateral institutions. When we analyse the politics of multilateral institutions in Chapter 4 and the future of multilateral institutions in Chapter 5, we also discuss what we define as the 'new' opposition to multilateral institutions and the 'politics of protest' around annual meetings (for example Seattle, Washington DC, Prague, Gothenburg and Genoa). Such mass protest has clearly made an impact on multilateral institutions, which are slowly starting to realise that reform is needed. The process of reform will necessarily involve civil society engagement, both through mass protests and targeted and critical dialogue. However, in order to have a positive and lasting impact, both types of civil society involvement must be built on a thorough understanding of the ways in which multilateral institutions actually operate. This is unfortunately not always the case. This book is therefore, we hope, a contribution in this regard.

MULTILATERALISM: A CRITICAL PERSPECTIVE

Since 1945 foreign policy has increasingly come to involve interstate arrangements such as the UN, the MDBs, the European Union (EU), the Group of Seven and a range of other multilateral arrangements. This trend has taken place to such an extent that several researchers within the field of international relations refer to the development of multilateralism (Scholte 2000). Multilateral responses have been generated to many of the challenges – both large and small – with which the world is faced. In this way, multilateralism has contributed to dissolving the distinction between *domestic* and *foreign* affairs, between the inside/outside, that is the hallmark of the Westphalian system.[1] There are, however, competing interpretations of what multilateralism is.

Broadly there are two different approaches: the 'rationalist' and the 'critical' (see Krause 2001). The rationalist view understands multilateralism as some sort of extension of self-interested interstate interaction. For authors such as Robert Keohane (1990: 732) and John G. Ruggie (1993: 11) multilateralism is 'an institutional form that co-ordinates relations among three or more states on the basis of generalized principles of conduct'. It is therefore different from bilateralism, a set of relations between two states, but also very different from imperialism, because it does not imply coordination between dominant and subordinate actors. This approach to multilateralism is state-centric and it treats states as autonomous and functionally equal actors operating in an international anarchy on the principles of self-interest. This rationalist view is broadly shared by both neorealists and institutionalists, although they disagree on whether multilateral institutions are merely a reflection of the distribution of power (neorealism) or whether, once established, they can have an independent effect on state behaviour (institutionalism).

A critical approach to multilateralism, on the other hand, which we favour, focuses more on the system rather than the totality of individual states, drawing attention to the underlying structures, forces and processes of world politics. This position has been developed by Robert Cox (1981, 1992 and 1997). Here, the evolution of multilateralism is seen as coexisting in a reciprocal relationship with global structural change. The critical approach therefore directs our attention toward the establishment of social order: a social order which is seen to be embedded in the nexus between material conditions, interests and ideas. A particular order is, under this interpretation, stabilised and perpetuated through 'institutionalisation'. Multilateral institutions thus reflect the power relations prevailing at their point of origin and tend, at least initially, to facilitate worldviews and beliefs (for instance in the merits of neoliberal economics) in accordance with these power relations. This implies that power relations are embedded in all multilateral institutions, even if these are supposedly based on diffuse reciprocity and formal equality among the member countries. Ideas play an important part in such an order, but, from this perspective, they are more than just reflections of the interests of the strongest members. Ideas also serve diverse social purposes and thereby also influence how member states define their interests in multilateral institutions (see Bøås and McNeill 2003). Thus, the multilateral institutions as such matter, and not just their member states. Outcomes are determined not simply by the distribution of power among the members that constitute the institution in question, but also by the multilateral institution itself, which can affect how choices are framed and outcomes reached. All multilateral institutions are also seen as social constructions: the product of particular historical circumstances. The actors involved are political, economic and social actors, operating not just through the state's foreign policy apparatus, but also transnationally. It is this perspective that we see as the most fruitful for what we call the 'critical engagement' approach to multilateral institutions.

Multilateral institutions as socially constructed arenas for the facilitation of international order

Multilateral institutions are social institutions, and social relations make or construct people (ourselves) into the kind of beings we are (see Onuf 1998). As Kratochwil and Ruggie (1986) put it, multilateral institutions are social institutions around which the experiences of actors converge. As such, multilateral institutions possess a clear coercive quality: 'Actors who enter into a social interaction rarely emerge the same' (Johnston 2001: 488). The member states and other actors in the institutions are expected to perform certain roles; the costs to actors who choose not to participate on these terms are uncertain and possibly very high.

All multilateral institutions are originally established in order to solve problems. After the completion of the reconstruction of Europe, the 'problem' was development (or the lack of it). President Truman's inaugural speech on 20 January 1949 is commonly held to mark the beginning of the modern development practice (Nustad 2003). In this speech, scientific and expert knowledge was packaged as the solution to poverty and misery:

We must embark on a bold new program for making the benefits of our scientific advances and industrial progress available for the improvement and growth of underdeveloped areas. More than half of the people of the world are living in conditions approaching misery. Their food is inadequate, they are victims of disease. Their economic life is primitive and stagnant. Their poverty is a handicap and threat both to them and more prosperous areas. For the first time in history, humanity possesses the knowledge and skill to relieve the suffering of these people ... our imponderable resources in the technical knowledge are constantly growing and are inexhaustible ... The old imperialism – exploitation for foreign profit – has no place in our plans ... Greater productivity is the key to prosperity and peace. And the key to greater production is wider and more vigorous application of modern scientific and technical knowledge. (quoted in Porter 1995: 66–7)

The means designed to resolve this problem were therefore the main tools of modernisation: 'scientific and technical knowledge'. The objective – increased prosperity and closer resemblance to Western societies – was the original goal of multilateral institutions, and despite all the new policies and approaches that have emerged subsequently this has remained at the heart of their activities.

What have been changed are the means, not the ends. And the changes that have taken place have been incremental, most often without any attempt to place new objectives in a logical, prior-itised order. The process of change that has taken place in multilateral institutions thus resembles what Ernst Haas has called 'change by adaptation' (see Haas 1990). In order to understand these processes it is important to bear in mind that multilateral institutions are intergovernmental organisations dominated by political groups (that is, country constituencies) whose behaviour often is subjected to bounded rationality because these groups also must balance between objectives, means, interests and ideas which are not necessarily coherent. This means that, in comparison to other social units, multilateral institutions confront rather special challenges when faced with, for instance, demands to incorporate new issue-areas. The mission of a multilateral institution is never simple and straightforward because both member states and other actors in their external environment may disagree on the interpretation of the mission (the ends) as well as on the tasks (the means) that need to be done if the mission is to be completed. In social units that function under such circumstances, organisational routines and standard operating procedures will be preferred to substantive change. Multilateral institutions will thus favour one particular way of arranging and routinising their activities. Since they have to satisfy different constituencies (that is, borrowing countries, donor countries and NGOs), multilateral institutions will try to avoid articulating explicitly competing views. Consensus therefore becomes an objective in itself, but the kind of consensus established in multilateral institutions is constructed on the power relationships prevailing in the institution in question. This means that consensus in multilateral institutions is usually artificial.

This way of reasoning also helps us to understand why the favoured approach of multilateral institutions in promoting development was that of the engineer. Development (or the lack of it) was seen as a technical issue, and not as a political question. If the challenges of development, and the new ideas supposed to resolve them, could be defined in technical terms, this increased the possibility of getting a proposal for action approved both by staff and by borrowing-country governments. Over time, a limited re-examination of the means utilised to reach their ends was made possible when new issue-areas were presented to the multilateral institutions in the same technocratic language as the old and familiar knowledge. By applying such a strategy of depoliticisation, new and potentially challenging discussions were kept within the framework of already existing standard operating procedures. It was therefore possible to treat potentially highly political questions, such as governance, as technical issues, and thereby the underlying political conflicts could, at least partly, be controlled. By this we mean the construction of artificial consensus on governance. If governance could be defined in strictly economic and technical terms, it would be easier to get acceptance for it as an issue-area for multilateral institutions.

Even though cross-cutting issue-areas such as poverty alleviation and sustainable development are supposedly prioritised issues for most multilateral institutions, they still argue for concentration of their grant and lending programmes in traditional sectors. Projects, however, should be modified by the inclusion of new social and environmental components and regulatory safeguards in order to ensure that environmental and social damage is avoided as much as possible. The approach of multilateral institutions is still clearly of an engineering problem-solving type, with policies and project papers written in the technical language that staff, management and Boards of multilateral institutions are used to.

In the 1950s and 1960s this strategy worked remarkably well. But in the 1970s and 1980s it was gradually called into question, and by the mid-1990s it was fully apparent that new development challenges could no longer be tackled by narrow technical approaches, and multilateral institutions started to experience more severe difficulties. The issue was no longer just a matter of finding the right technical solution to a functional problem. Today, the challenge is to construct some sort of consensus around an increasingly politicised agenda constituted around a whole range of new cross-cutting themes such as governance, involuntary resettlement, and indigenous peoples. Clearly, the technocratic consensus on development has reached its limits. It is no longer in any credible way possible to define development solely in a technical and functional manner. As a consequence, the internal artificial consensus is disappearing, not only between donor and borrowing member countries of multilateral institutions, but also internally in these institutions. An increasingly political agenda will make the process of political manoeuvring between donor and recipient countries and other stakeholders (civil societies and the private sectors) increasingly difficult for multilateral institutions. A critical perspective on multilateralism can help in revealing and understanding the interplay between the underlying forces and processes of multilateralism and how these are linked by reciprocity to structures of global change.

Critical engagement

Our perspective is therefore based on two pillars that we perceive as closely connected. One is concerned with how and why the policies and approaches of multilateral institutions came into existence. In order to ask such questions, we need to understand both the historical processes that led to the establishment of these institutions in the first place, and how the structures underlying the particular world order that these institutions represent has changed over time. Crucial in this regard is the gradual dominance of the neoliberal economic paradigm. However, there is much more to these processes than just the prominence of neoliberal-ism. Certain actors have not only promoted this paradigm, but also used it for the purpose of facilitating specific strategic interests. The role of the United States, and in particular the US Treasury Department, is significant in this context. Nevertheless, we cannot explain multilateral institutions by just referring to neoliberalism and the US Treasury Department. Both constitute important elements of explanations, but are far from the whole story. Both structures and agents are important, and there is a multitude of actors involved in these institutions. NGOs and social movements have played a substantial role in these processes, sometimes in opposition, sometimes in alliance with specific states or internal actors in the multilateral institution(s) concerned. In some cases smaller member states such as the so-called 'like-minded countries' have played an important part. And the responses and relative influence of different borrowing member countries is very varied; they differ both between countries and multilateral institutions. It is not easy to conceptualise power within this system. As well as being related to material resources, power can also be ideational. Also, although being an important contributor (such as the United States) gives power and influence, a big borrower can also have considerable influence. Here, we must remember that the World Bank and the regional development banks are *banks*, and what kind of customer does a bank prefer? They prefer customers who borrow a lot of money and repay their loans on time. A good customer country such as China gains influence precisely by being the kind of customer that all banks – development banks included – like to have as their client. One pillar of our critical engagement perspective is therefore a research programme whose aim is to investigate the internal politics of multilateral institutions – as it evolves in the interplay between member states, the institution itself, and NGOs. Multilateral institutions should not be treated as unitary actors.

While this is the 'critical' element of our approach, the other is 'engagement': a desire to contribute to improvement – one which is based on sober, but critical analyses of the politics, procedures and approaches of multilateral institutions. The policies and approaches of multilateral institutions are of crucial importance for the well-being of millions of people. Yet, in our view (a view apparently shared by many others) these institutions are not functioning as they should. Substantial reform is needed. The current state of poverty and environmental degradation in the world should in itself be evidence that the technical and functional approach has not been a success. Development is a political process and should be treated as such by multilateral institutions. To pretend that it is not, as these institutions still continue to do, is merely a facade, and on this facade only an artificial consensus can be built. The mass protests around the annual meetings of multilateral institutions suggest that more and more people see through this facade, and as a result the credibility of multilateral institutions is reduced even more. We do not argue for these institutions to be closed down. We believe that multilateral institutions are necessary for all, not least the poor and the powerless. But if they are to fulfil their role, the institutions must be reformed. Such reform will require engagement by many interested parties. But this engagement must be built on an understanding of the ways in which the system of multilateral institutions actually operates that is informed by a critical perspective. If not, we fear that attempts at reform will be like building castles in the sand before a high tide.

THE STRUCTURE OF THIS BOOK

The multilateral institutions are complex and they perform a range of different roles. There is no shortage of technical information concerning them: their financing, lending and impact (see 'Internet Resources', pp. 168–9). What we will try to present here is a concise and coherent introduction which focuses on the key aspects of these institutions that are important for an understanding of the politics of their functioning. We will concentrate on what we consider to be their main features, and these we will present in a non-specialised language. Language is power, and in multilateral institutions a language has been developed which clearly alienates ordinary citizens from gaining insight into what is actually going on in, for example, the World Bank and the IMF. One important task is therefore to offer an analysis that shows what is happening in these institutions, to people who have not spent years working with them or studying them. In order to achieve this, we have organised the book into five chapters, each building on the previous ones. Our critical engagement perspective is integrated throughout.

In Chapter 2, we describe how multilateral institutions operate: how they are financed and how they distribute resources through grants and loans. We analyse how they are organised, and in particular we are concerned with how member countries are organised into country constituencies. We look at the basic distinction between donor and recipient countries, and also identify which are the most powerful actors within the institutions concerned. Multilateral institutions also interact with each other, and we here address the relationships between key actors like the World Bank, the UNDP and the regional development banks, and to a lesser degree the relationship between these key actors and the IMF and the WTO. The three major functions of multilateral institutions – project assistance, programme lending and policy advice – are also considered, and how these relate to the doctrine of political neutrality. Strategies of depoliticisation and the role of economics constitute crucial elements in this analysis.

The changing policies of multilateral institutions are the theme of Chapter 3. Here we return in-depth to the three major roles of multilateral institutions, and we start by describing the broadening that has taken place in these institutions' agendas. They all started from a very narrow project-oriented approach to development. The process of development was seen through the eyes of an engineer, and economic growth was the key concept behind their activities. Economic growth is still viewed by these institutions as the means to development and the defeat of poverty, but this concept no longer stands alone in the headlines of these institutions. Particularly from the end of the 1980s and onwards, it has been supplemented by issues of sustainable development, good governance, participatory approaches to development, indigenous peoples, involuntary resettlement, etc. In that respect their agenda has been broadened significantly. Nevertheless, closer scrutiny of the policies and approaches of these institutions reveal that the changes that have taken place are incremental. On a superficial level, it may seem as if the World Bank and the other multilateral institutions have travelled a long distance from project assistance to good governance. However, when we start to analyse these changes critically it becomes evident that the reforms that have taken place have not substantially challenged the old technical and functional approach to development in these institutions. The reforms and the new policies adopted so far have not led these institutions into a self-reflective mood which would entail a radical re-examination of purpose. To a considerable degree they still operate under old standard operating procedures and organisational routines. Development (and lack of it) is still mainly addressed as a technical issue.

There are reasons for this, and these reasons we start to discover when we begin unpacking the 'black box' of multilateral institutions in Chapter 4. Here we see the interplay between member states, the institutions themselves, and actors in their external environment such as the NGOs. We start by drawing up the general picture of this interplay. How do the three sets of actors operate? What are the rules that frame this relationship and how regular is their interaction? In order to illustrate these general arguments we here draw on a set of case studies, based on internal policy papers, loan decisions and personal experience with multilateral institutions both in the field and at their headquarters and annual meetings. These include the Pelosi Amendment in the US, the Arun III Hydro-power project in Nepal and the Samut Prakarn Wastewater Management project in Thailand. These cases also highlight both the potential and the challenges involved in civil society participation in processes such as this. Questions concerning both legitimacy and representation will be asked, and we will also consider the relationship between powerful international NGOs and local NGOs. Finally, this chapter will also be concerned with what we define as the 'new' opposition to multilateral institutions and the 'politics of protest' around annual meetings. The combined IMF/World Bank annual meetings in Madrid in 1994, the 'Fifty Years is Enough' campaign and the organisation of the Madrid Alternative Forum were the first real attempts to create mass protests against multilateral institutions. As civil protests these events are quite standard: people shout slogans, carry posters and sometimes are beaten by the police and sometimes attack the police. What is new is the sophisticated global organisation of protest prior to the meetings, and the diverse crowd who take part in the protest. The event in Seattle in November 1999 during the WTO Ministerial Meeting was the first and perhaps also foremost example of this sophistication and diversity, but the same pattern repeated itself in Washington DC, Prague and Chiang Mai in 2000, and in Gothenburg and Genoa in 2001. These demonstrations included everything from anarchists, represented by the Black Bloc and Ya Basta to organisations interested in dialogue and reform like Friends of the Earth, the World Wildlife Fund (WWF) and BothEnds. This has created a particular kind of politics of protest around these annual meetings. The chapter will specify the characteristics of this politics of protest, and what kind of civil society response we can therefore expect.

In the final part of this book, in Chapter 5, we will discuss the future of these institutions. Will some sort of reformed neoliberalism become the new vantage point of multilateral institutions or will a new version of social corporatism take its place? Will we in future be confronted with a much more thoroughgoing privatisation of the multilateral system than that implied by the still rather limited inflow of private finance that we can observe today? And what about the role of the United States? Currently we are seeing increased unilateralism displayed by the Bush II administration, which later is dressed up as multilateralism. Are we heading towards an era of uni-Americanism? What implications will such developments have for new issue-areas and linkages in the early twenty-first century, and for the organisation of the multilateral system as a whole? One important question is whether we will come to experience increased regionalisation of the multilateral system. Another is whether we will see increased engagement between civil society and multilateral institutions. What will happen to the broad coalition involved in mass protest towards institutions like the World Bank? Will it prove sustainable or will it splinter into a coopted wing (the voice of acceptable opposition) seeking only minimal reform, and a radical wing, seeking confrontation? We hope and argue for a middle way, based on critical engagement.

CONCLUDING REMARKS

The current state of the multilateral system is clearly far from perfect, and is in need of major reform. But it is important to recognise that multilateralism constitutes some kind of protection for the weak and the poor. Multilateral institutions do place some constraints on the activity of strong powers and thereby also offer some protection for weaker actors. Although powerful countries are also powerful in multilateral institutions, that does not mean that they make all the decisions. For small states and poor countries (and people), multilateralism is surely preferable to unilateralism. It is important that we keep this in mind when we discuss multilateral institutions. We believe that what are needed are strong, not weak multilateral institutions. But the strong multilateral system which we would like to see is one in which critical perspectives and viewpoints are encouraged, not repressed; and where such views – based on informed, critical analysis – have an impact on the governance of the system and the decisions that are taken in the name of all the member countries.

2
The Stuctural Design of Multilateral Institutions

The World Bank is only one of many multilateral institutions that claim to operate in the public interest. Officially, the multilateral development banks (MDBs) (that is, the regional development banks and the World Bank) are accountable only to their member states, whose votes are weighted according to their respective financial contributions. However, a varying degree of autonomy of Bank managers and staff *vis-à-vis* the formal owners of the MDBs (the member states) is widely recognised. One piece of evidence is that the Board of the World Bank has never rejected a loan proposal from management (Fox and Brown 2000a). Even if the MDBs were effectively accountable to their member governments, many critics would still reject such a formal criterion for accountability due to the fact that votes are distributed according to a *one dollar, one vote* system. In fact, when one leaves this formal institutional domain, the relationship between the actors involved in the making of multilateral development policy is often unclear, more characterised by informal practice than formal rules and guidelines.

THE BRETTON WOODS INSTITUTIONS

In July 1944, representatives from 45 countries gathered at Bretton Woods, New Hampshire in the United States to devise a stable global economic system that would avert calamities such as the Great Depression and its lingering effects, which had culminated in the Second World War. The anchors of the 'Bretton Woods System' were the IMF and the International Bank for Reconstruction and Development (IBRD). The latter is today better known as the World Bank. The IMF was charged with providing a stable international monetary system that would promote trade while the IBRD was to aid in the reconstruction of Western Europe, essentially by channelling US money to European development. Subsequently, five major regional development banks came into being: two in Europe and one each in the Americas, Africa and Asia. (The European Investment Bank (EIB) was established in 1958, the IDB in 1959, the African Development Bank (AfDB) and the Asian Development Bank (ADB) in 1964, and the European Bank for Reconstruction and Development (EBRD) in 1990.)

The MDBs represent a form of international cooperation the world had not seen prior to 1945, an evolution from the League of Nations and UN models, in which all member countries formally have an equal voice and vote. Their structure is inspired by the joint-stock model of private capitalist corporations, in which member countries are shareholders whose voting powers vary with their relative economic importance. In other words, each member country's share of the votes is weighted in accordance with the combined amount of capital it has paid in and is guaranteeing for. That said, the MDBs institutional design is also inspired by the logic of the MDBs' basic mandate which is to act as intermediaries between private international capital markets and the governments of developing countries.

THE WORLD BANK

Established in 1944, the World Bank is the world's largest provider of development assistance. It is involved in more than a hundred countries, and in 2001, the total World Bank loans to its client countries amounted to US$17.6 billion. Formally, the World Bank is owned by its 180 member countries whose views and interests are to be represented by a Board of Governors and a Washington-based Board of Directors. Both recipient and donor countries are shareholders, and they are therefore supposed to be jointly exercising ultimate decision-making power in the World Bank. The main governing body of the World Bank is the Board of Governors. Each member state appoints a governor, who is entitled to cast the number of votes the country represents, with issues formally decided by majority. However, in practice consensus is the norm at the Board of Governors' meetings. Among other responsibilities the Board of Governors is in charge of the presidential election, changes in the World Bank's capital stock, the establishment of special funds and the approval of the annual financial statements of the institution. However, since the Board of Governors usually only meets once a year, at the annual meeting, most of their authority has *de facto* been delegated to the Board of Directors. The Executive Directors (EDs) serve on the Board of Directors and they are the resident representatives in Washington of the member governments. The EDs are entrusted with the responsibility of supervising the general operations of the World Bank. They discuss loan proposals, new programme initiatives and policy papers. At the Board of Directors political controversy is more visible than at the Board of Governors, although here it is also very rare that votes are actually cast. This does not imply that votes do not matter. They do, but consensus is often achieved by weaker countries modifying their policy positions in accordance with those of stronger countries. This means that the consensus produced by the World Bank is often quite artificial. It is not necessarily seen as legitimate by all member countries, as may be illustrated by policy debates concerning sustainable development, and good governance (see Chapter 3).

The president of the World Bank, currently James Wolfensohn, is the chairman of the Board. He constitutes a key component in the World Bank's institutional governance structure. He is allowed to vote in the event of a tie at the Board, but much more important is his role as chairperson. Since votes are rarely used, it is most often left to the president to interpret the degree of consensus and then draw the conclusions. And as the World Bank's legal representative, he is responsible not only for daily business carried out under the management of the EDs, but also for World Bank organisation, staff matters and the implementation of policy decisions. The president is the formal link between Board decisions and World Bank behaviour.

The Board of Directors consists of 24 EDs. Five countries have permanent representation at the Board, and these countries appoint their EDs directly (see Table 2.1).

Table 2.1   World Bank permanent Board members (and votes as of 17 September 2001)[1]

Country	Number of votes	Per cent of total
United States	1,865,737	14.45
Japan	1,414,996	10.96
Germany	913,474	7.08
United Kingdom	641,302	4.97
France	561,248	4.35

The remaining 175 member countries are organised in country constituencies – each with an ED, an alternative ED, and Director's Assistants from the other member countries. In most country constituencies, the executive directorship is rotated every three or four years, and when one country holds the directorship, the other countries usually play a more passive role. Generally, the ED in place makes decisions based on consultations with the home office (usually the foreign affairs or finance ministry) and the home office of other country constituency members. One example of such a country constituency is the Nordic-Baltic Office in the World Bank. This is the country constituency of Denmark, Estonia, Finland, Iceland, Latvia, Lithuania, Norway and Sweden. The ED of this country constituency controls 4.94 per cent of total votes. In some country constituencies, one country informally holds the executive directorship permanently. This is usually the case when one country holds a much larger share of the total votes than the other country constituency members. One example is the country constituency composed of Barbados, Belize, Canada, Dominica, Grenada, Guyana, Ireland, St. Kitts and Nevis, St. Lucia and St. Vincent & The Grenadines. In this group Canada is the dominant country, controlling more than double the votes of the rest of the constituency members. Thus, *de facto*, Canada is also a permanent Board member. This means that we have three different types of country constituencies:

- single-member constituencies,
- multi-member constituencies, with permanent executive directorship, and
- multi-member constituencies, with rotating executive directorship.

Capital construction, financing and lending

The capital construction of all MDBs was established with the formation of the World Bank. From the outset, the World Bank was designed to be an institution which was to be owned, and whose capital would be provided, by governments and not by private sources. Its initial authorised capitalisation of US$10 billion consisted of 20 per cent in the form of paid-in capital and 80 per cent in the form of callable or guaranteed capital. This distinction is crucial for our understanding of the multilateral system at large.

Each country subscription to the World Bank and the other MDBs is divided into two parts. The larger one is the so-called *callable capital*. This amount of money is not actually paid by the member states to the World Bank or any other MDB, but each member country guarantees for a certain sum of money. The credit rating of the World Bank and the other MDBs is based on the amount of capital guaranteed for by the rich industrialised countries. The *paid-in capital* is the much smaller amount of money that each country actually pays to the World Bank. Each member state's percentage of votes is based on the weighting of each country's total contribution of paid-in and callable capital. The rich countries' total contribution of paid-in and callable capital is much larger than that of the developing member countries. This is the main reason why the United Kingdom, for example, controls 4.94 per cent of the votes in the World Bank's concessional window, whereas a developing country like Tanzania controls only 0.28 per cent.

All MDBs except the EBRD provide financing to developing member countries through two windows. The 'hard window' comes closest to the functions of an ordinary bank: it provides nonconcessional loans (that is, financing at market rates of interest) with maturities (repayment periods) up to 20 years. Such long maturities are almost unknown among commercial banks; thus even in this respect the MDBs differ from conventional banks. The funds from these loans are obtained through the MDBs' own borrowing on international capital markets, which is usually effected through the issuance of bonds or similar instruments. The nonconcessional window of the World Bank is the IBRD, which provides loans and development assistance to middle-income countries and creditworthy poorer countries.

The World Bank's bonds, which are offered in all major capital markets (and hence generate loanable funds in many different currencies), have typically attracted the highest possible credit ratings (AAA) from credit-rating agencies such as Moody's, Fitch and Standard & Poor's. This signifies to bond investors that they are top-quality investments and virtually risk-free.[2] Such ratings mean that the World Bank's own cost of borrowing (or the interest paid to their bondholders) is at the lowest level possible in the market; therefore, the funds can be made available to the MDBs' borrowers at the lowest possible interest costs. The MDBs maintain their high credit ratings because their borrowing is 100 per cent secured by capital paid-in or guaranteed by the member countries (or, to be more precise, predominantly the rich member countries). Loans are usually offered on much better terms than developing countries could obtain on their own from the international capital market. To illustrate, it is cheaper for a country like Namibia to borrow money from the World Bank than to go by itself directly to international capital markets. It is with countries as with people: the less affluent you are, the higher interest you will have to pay in order to get a loan from a private bank. Still, MDBs generally extend nonconcessional loans only to countries deemed to be creditworthy (that is, able to repay the loan).

Only a small portion of the capital subscriptions of member countries is actually paid-in (between 3 and 5 per cent in recent capital replenishments). The rest is subject to call (and is therefore referred to either as callable capital or guaranteed capital). Such calls have never been made, and all those concerned – shareholders, the World Bank and the other MDBs themselves and the capital markets – assume no call ever will be made. This convention is important for the structure and functioning of the World Bank because it enables shareholders to take large equity positions without correspondingly large cash outlays, and the large equity stake of shareholders enables the World Bank to secure commensurately large borrowings (with a maximum gearing ratio of 1:1, a dollar of debt for each dollar of equity) on the capital markets. Investors who purchase World Bank and other MDB bonds in the capital markets regard the capital structure of these institutions as a mechanism for securing their obligations against what amounts to a guarantee by shareholders to pay any amounts necessary up to the full value of bonds outstanding. In other words, the servicing – and high credit rating – of World Bank and other MDBs' bonds are dependent on the implicit guarantee of the shareholders rather than on the loan repayments of the developing-country borrowers that ultimately obtain the funds.

In contrast to the 'hard window', the 'soft window' provides concessional loans (often called credits, which carry rates of interest considerably below market levels, typically close to zero) to the poorest countries. Even though the transactions involve low-interest loans rather than grants, this function is more similar to that of an aid agency than of a bank. In fact, the resources for soft loans come from the aid budgets of the major donor countries, which meet every three years to negotiate replenishments for the 'soft windows' of the World Bank and other MDBs. These funds form a significant portion of the overall flow of aid to developing countries, and in particular to the least developed countries which are not seen as creditworthy enough to obtain loans from the 'hard windows' of the World Bank and other MDBs. The 'soft window' of the World Bank – the International Development Association (IDA) – was established in 1960. The IDA is important because it represents the first acknowledgement from the World Bank that the development enterprise was more complex than its founding fathers originally had envisioned; involving not simply the financing of infrastructure over a limited period.

The IDA provides financial resources and technical assistance to about 80 countries. These countries have little or no access to market-based financing, and the vast majority of their people live on less than US$2 a day. The major client continent for the IDA is Africa.

In the 1990s, obtaining funding for the IDA and other development funds (the 'soft window' of the AfDB, ADB and the IDB) met with serious obstacles in the US Congress, which refused to honour, among other things, commitments made by the US administration under the 10th Replenishment (IDA-10). During the 1990s this was a continuing problem, and these difficult negotiations have thrown into doubt the future of the soft-loan facilities of the MDBs. The main reason is that the recipients of these facilities, particularly in Africa, are predominantly the poorest countries whose needs for foreign assistance are not declining. At the same time, many of the traditional Asian and Latin American borrowers from the regular (hard-loan) facilities of the MDBs are increasingly able to access private capital markets.

The problem is that the World Bank and the other MDBs are ill suited to face the challenges that confront them; they have a surfeit of nonconcessional resources for advanced developing countries that need them less (or only when a major crisis emerges such as the Asian financial crisis of 1997) and are faced with a shortage of concessional resources for the poorest countries that need those resources more than ever. On the other hand, as the World Bank and the other MDBs mature, their role as banks assumes greater importance in the mobilisation of resources. Since most MDB assistance has been provided not as grants but as loans (at both near-market and lower rates of interest), repayments are providing a growing source of funding for new loans. Thus, the MDBs are experiencing a greater degree of funding autonomy, just as their main member countries' willingness or ability to provide them with additional funding is decreasing.

The United States and the World Bank

The dominance of the United States is crucial to understanding both the establishment and early development of the World Bank, and the policies it pursued in the 1980s and 1990s. The multilateral institution which emerged out of the Bretton Woods conference was firstly an American creation, secondly Anglo-Saxon, and only thirdly an international institution. The United States supplied most of the resources necessary for making loans and was also by far the predominant market for Bank securities.

Over the years there have been two conflicting opinions of US influence on the World Bank. One, held by many members of the US Congress, argues that the United States has too little influence on what the World Bank does. The World Bank, it is claimed, is run by highly paid, aloof bureaucrats, unresponsive to US concerns and accountable only to themselves. The opposite view, held by substantial numbers of World Bank staff, and many outsiders – most notably NGO groups in borrowing countries and other member countries – maintains that the World Bank is run by the United States. A more sober analysis supports neither of these extreme positions. Our view is that the US influence on the World Bank is important, but not absolute.

Nevertheless, throughout the history of the World Bank, the United States has been the largest shareholder and the most influential member country. US support for, pressures on, and criticism of the World Bank have been central to its growth and the evolution of its policies, programmes and practices. Underlying this half-century of US–World Bank relations has been a fundamental ambivalence on the part of the United States toward both development assistance and multilateral cooperation in general (see Gwin 1994). US support for the World Bank has been based on the view that promoting economic growth and development in other parts of the world is in the national interest and that multilateral cooperation is a particularly effective way of both leveraging and allocating resources for development purposes that serve the national interest of the US. The US Treasury Department has consistently emphasised these points. The United States has viewed all multilateral institutions, including the World Bank, as instruments of foreign policy to be used in support of specific US aims and objectives. Thus, while various US administrations have supported the World Bank for its capacity as a multilateral institution to leverage funds and influence borrowing countries' economic policies, the United States has been uneasy with the autonomy on which the development role of the World Bank (and the other regional development banks) depends, and the power sharing that accompanies burden sharing.

This ambivalence, a preoccupation with containing communism, and the change in relative US power in the world, explain much of the evolution in the US's relations with the World Bank over the past decades. The US Congress, unlike the legislators in other member countries, has been a major influence on World Bank policy. Within the context of changing foreign policy concerns, congressional involvement has significantly affected the style and approach of US participation in the World Bank. Having promoted the establishment, early financial growth and expansion of the World Bank's programme, the US in the 1970s often found itself at odds with the Bank. The debt crisis in the South (in particular in Latin America) and the collapse of the Soviet Union's sphere of influence in Eastern Europe led to renewed US interest in the World Bank, at the same time as pressure from NGOs caused the US government to push it to be more environmentally aware. However, renewed US attention to the World Bank was accompanied in the 1980s and 1990s by both a continuing decrease in the US share of World Bank funding and a unilateral, dogmatic assertiveness on matters of World Bank policies, a combination that antagonised several other member countries (both donor and recipient). Especially since the 1980s, the US Congress has used its power of the purse to direct and restrict US financial participation in the World Bank.

In order to understand the relationship between the World Bank and the US, we should start by acknowledging that foreign aid has never been popular in Congress. Although objections were muted in the years just after the Second World War, Congress quickly became dissatisfied with it and distrustful of multilateral institutions. As a consequence, most members of Congress were uninterested and uninformed about World Bank operations. Even on key committees there was much misunderstanding of what the World Bank did and how it operated (see Schoultz 1982). The increased appropriation requests therefore became attractive targets. Over time there has also been a breakdown of discipline and effective leadership in Congress, making it increasingly difficult to manoeuvre unpopular aid requests through the labyrinthine authorisation and appropriation procedures. No fewer than five committees have significant jurisdiction over US policy towards the World Bank. The most important ones are the House Banking Sub-committee on International Development Institutions and Finance, and the Appropriations Subcommittee of Foreign Relations.

This kind of institutional arrangement provides multiple entry points for interest groups with specific policy agendas (for instance, environmental NGOs), and it creates a situation in which strategically placed members of Congress, and specific issues, may gain disproportionate weight in the policy process. As long as Congress was passive in making US policy towards the World Bank, its basic dislike of foreign aid and multilateral institutions and its cumbersome legislative procedures were of limited significance. But as it became less deferential on matters of foreign policy, these factors became formative for US policy towards, and participation in, the World Bank.

The basis of US influence therefore derives, on the most fundamental level, from the origins of the World Bank and the fact that its Charter and guiding principles have a distinctly American cast. It is American thinking about the roles of government and markets that provides the conceptual centre of gravity for World Bank debates, rather than that of Europe, Japan or the developing countries. Over the years, the United States has used its influence to ensure that those principles are not disregarded. Other sources of US influence include its position as the largest shareholder in the World Bank, the importance of its financial market as a source of capital for the World Bank (and other MDBs), and its hold on the position of the presidency of the World Bank and other senior management positions, reinforced by the World Bank's location in Washington. The great majority of World Bank economists, whatever their nationality, have a postgraduate qualification from a North American university. And there are many subtle ways in which the Bank's location – in the heart of Washington DC, just a few blocks from the White House, US Treasury and Washington-based think-tanks – helps contribute to the way in which American premises structure the very mindset of most World Bank staff, who read American newspapers, watch American television and use American English as their *lingua franca* (Wade 2001). Although its relative importance in many of these dimensions has declined, the United States remains the dominant member country in the World Bank, in large part because no other country or group of countries (such as the EU or Japan) has chosen to deliberately challenge it (see Table 2.2).

Table 2.2   US voting shares in the World Bank, 1950–2000

	1950	1960	1970	1980	1990	2001
US	34.1	30.3	24.5	21.1	15.1	16.45

The only member country or group of countries that has really tried to challenge some of the underlying premises that the United States seeks to protect and promote in the Bank is Japan. These challenges took place in the few years of Asia-euphoria, just prior to the emergence of the Asian financial crisis in 1997. At the centre of this debate was the role of the state in development. Particularly since the 1980s the World Bank has endorsed the principle of the self-adjusting market: the necessity of 'getting the prices right' and providing a 'level playing field'. These principles are deeply embedded in the neoliberal economic ideology which emerged in the US and Britain during the 1980s. The dominant ideology was that one set of rules should apply to all countries, and the major representation of these rules was the idea that the proper role of the state was to provide the framework for private sector activity in a financial system based on private capital.

Prior to the arrival of the Reagan administration in Washington, Japan had few quarrels with the American emphasis on the merits of market forces, privatisation and liberalisation. However, during the 1980s, Japan increasingly questioned the neoliberal model, and particularly its appropriateness for Asia. The Japanese government and especially the Ministry of Finance (MOF) resented what they interpreted as inflexible American attempts to apply neoliberal economic principles to Asian countries that lacked a strong private sector tradition, and benefited from government intervention in the economy (Bøås 2001a).[3] This critique reflected Japan's own experience as a developmental state with a state-controlled, bank-based financial system. Thus, in the late 1980s and early 1990s, Japan began to use its financial muscle to take on a more active role in the multilateral system: not simply adapting but also debating. Their objective was to modify the approach of the World Bank and other MDBs so as to be more in line with the economic systems of Japan and East Asia. In response to intense Japanese pressure over an extended period of time, the World Bank agreed to conduct a study of the causes of economic growth in East Asia. The US Treasury was opposed to the idea of doing such a study, but when Japan promised to pay for the whole study agreement was finally reached.

The study cost the Japanese government more than US$1.2 million and for Japan and other East Asian countries who had hoped that it would contribute to renewed reflections in the World Bank about the role of the state, the conclusion was a huge disappointment. According to the World Bank's *East Asian Miracle Report* (1993), the lessons to be learnt from East Asia had no implications for the World Bank's approach to development; rather, a careful analysis of what had taken place in East Asia confirmed the validity of their position on the role of the state. As Wade put it in his critical commentary on the World Bank's approach:

> Through the 1980s, the Bank had pressed the view that the central problem of developing countries is that they provided only a weak 'enabling environment' for private-sector growth: they failed to provide adequate infrastructure, macroeconomic stability, a framework of law and property rights, transparency in policy-making and universal primary education. *The East Asian Miracle* finds that the presence of such an enabling environment in East Asia is the main explanation of the region's superior performance. Conversely, selective industrial policies fortunately turn out to have been largely ineffective, despite the popular image of these countries as champions of industrial policy. (Wade 1994: 56)

One may well argue that this was the only conclusion possible for the World Bank: if industrial policy had emerged from the study as the main explanation of East Asia's economic success, both the World Bank's message and its image as the intellectual leader of the development debate would have been significantly damaged. To critical observers it was obvious that the World Bank could not tolerate any other conclusion, because that would entail that what the World Bank had been preaching to its client countries for the past decade had been wrong. It was argued that the conclusions of the report had been tailor-made to fit with the worldview of the US Treasury. The debate continued in the World Bank and several other agencies across the multilateral system, until the Asian financial crisis in 1997 dealt a devastating blow to Japanese and Asian challenges to the United States in the World Bank. European Union coordination is slowly becoming more evident in both the World Bank and other MDBs, but so far this group has neither been willing nor able to challenge the dominant position of the United States within these institutions. One possible scenario, to which we will return in more detail in Chapters 4 and 5, is that the new unilateralism ('uni-Americanism') of the Bush II administration will provoke a more unified European approach and also a European–Asian alliance.

THE INTERNATIONAL MONETARY FUND

The establishment of the IMF resulted from lengthy discussions of four alternative proposals – American, British, Canadian and French – during the Second World War. The British Keynes Plan proposed an international clearing union that would create an international means of payment called 'bancor'. The rival American plan, named after Harry Dexter White from the US Treasury, instead proposed a currency pool to which members would make specified contributions only, and from which countries might borrow in order to help themselves over short-term balance-of-payments deficits. Both plans envisioned a political economy more or less free of controls imposed for balance-of-payments purposes. Common to both plans was the attainment of exchange-rate stability without a return to the international gold standard, and the maintenance of substantial national autonomy in monetary and fiscal policies. According to conventional wisdom, the major difference was that the Keynes Plan emphasised national autonomy, whereas the White Plan considered exchange-rate stability to be of prime importance.

The Articles of Agreement of the IMF, like those of its sister institution the World Bank, were drafted and signed at the Bretton Woods conference in 1944. By the end of 1945, enough countries had ratified the agreement to bring the IMF into existence. The Board of Governors first met in March 1946, adopted by-laws and decided to locate the headquarters in Washington DC. One year later the IMF started to operate.

The IMF's primary task was to monitor and manage a system of stable exchange rates in which the value of all currencies was based on gold and the US dollar. In order to ensure the stability of this system, the US government guaranteed the value of the dollar in gold at a set rate of US$35 per ounce. This system was to be the basis for international trade, which was considered the engine of economic growth and prosperity.

The IMF's second major function was to provide countries with short-term financing from its vast reserves of foreign currencies and gold to help them overcome temporary balance-of-payments deficits and support their exchange-rate values. These reserves came from the contributions by IMF founding members, based on the size of their economy. Up until the United States abandoned the gold standard in 1971, due to inflationary pressure and the costs of the war it was fighting in Vietnam, these were the two major functions of the IMF. After President Nixon unilaterally abandoned the gold standard, the main responsibility of the IMF has been short-term loans for balance-of-payments deficits.

The IMF: organisation, financing and lending

Currently more than 180 countries are members of the IMF. Formally, membership is open to any country that conducts its own foreign policy, and is willing to adhere to the IMF charter of rights and obligations. All major economies are members of the IMF. On joining, each member country contributes a certain amount of money called a quota subscription, quite similar to a credit union deposit. These quotas serve different purposes:

- They form a pool of money that the IMF can draw from to lend to member countries in financial difficulties.
- They are the basis for determining how much money a member country can borrow from the IMF or receive from the IMF in periodic allocations (known as special drawing

rights). The more a member contributes, the more it can borrow in time of need.

- They determine the voting power of the member.

The IMF, based on an analysis of each country's wealth and economic performance, sets the amount of the quota the member will contribute: the more affluent the country, the higher the quota. Quotas are reviewed every five years and they can be raised or lowered both according to the needs of the IMF and the economic prosperity of the member in question (see Table 2.3).

Table 2.3   Largest quotas and votes as of 5 March 2002[4]

Country	Total votes	Per cent of Fund total
United States	371,743	17.16
Japan	133,378	6.16
Germany	130,332	6.02
France	107,635	4.97
United Kingdom	107,635	4.97

Table 2.3 shows the quotas and voting power of the five largest shareholder countries. (For the sake of comparison, the African country with the largest quota is South Africa, which holds 0.87 per cent of the total.) As is the case in the World Bank, the remaining member countries are organised in country constituencies. Some have a permanent executive directorship, whereas others rotate this role among the members of the constituency.

Formally, the IMF is not granted very much autonomy. The chain of command is supposed to run directly from the governments of member countries to the IMF. Thus, when the IMF works out lending arrangements, including conditionalities, the IMF formally acts not on its own, but as an intermediary between the will of the majority of the membership and the individual member country. However, it is very clear that those who contribute the most to IMF (see Table 2.3) are also given the strongest voice in determining policies. This means that the IMF, if it is an intermediary, is an intermediary between the strongest economies in the world and individual member countries, and not necessarily between the majority and the individual.

Just as in the case of the World Bank, the IMF has a Board of Governors, and a Board of Directors which comprises the resident representatives in Washington. As of March 2002 the Board consisted of 24 EDs. It is very rare that the Board makes its decisions on the basis of formal voting. As in the World Bank, the usual procedure is the formation of consensus among the Board members. Here also, however, this is an artificial consensus constructed on the basis of the distribution of power among the Board members.

The quota subscriptions (or membership fees as we may also call them) constitute the largest source of funds for the IMF. However, as each member has the right to borrow from the IMF several times the amount it has paid in as a membership fee, quotas may not provide enough cash to fully meet the borrowing needs of members in a period of great stress in the world economy. The Asian financial crisis of 1997 is one example. This is why the so-called 'general arrangements to borrow' was established already in 1962. In reality, this arrangement is a line of credit with a number of governments and banks throughout the world. This is renewed every five years, and the IMF pays interest on whatever it borrows under these arrangements, and undertakes to repay the loan in five years. The actual system for raising funds is different from the one we found in the World Bank, but the principle is the same. Both institutions borrow money on international capital markets based on the money paid in and guaranteed for, first and foremost by its most affluent member countries.

The IMF is not a development institution *per se* like the World Bank. Its mission is much narrower. It only lends to member countries with payments problems, that is, to countries that do not earn enough foreign currency to pay for what they buy from others. In a capitalist political economy, the same logic applies for countries as for people. A country, just like a person, can spend far more than it earns, making up the difference – at least for a time – by borrowing; but sooner or later its credit will be exhausted. When this happens, things usually get unpleasant.[5] For a country, the result is a loss in the buying power of its currency and thereby also a forced reduction in the volume of its imports from other countries. In such a situation, a country that is a member of the IMF can turn to that institution for assistance. The IMF will for a time lend it foreign exchange, a loan which is supposed to help the country in question to reform its economy, stabilising its currency and strengthening its trade. Particularly in Africa this has proven to be more in theory than in practice. Many African countries have rolled from one short-term rescue package to another.

Any member country with a payment problem has the right to immediately withdraw from the IMF the 25 per cent of its quota that it paid in gold or a convertible currency. If this is not enough, a member may request more money from the IMF and can over a period of years borrow cumulatively three times what it paid in as a quota subscription. This limit does not apply to loans under IMF's special facilities. Among these is the supplementary reserve facility (SRF), created during the Asian financial crisis. The SRF provides short-term financing to members faced with a sudden and disruptive loss of financial market confidence. South Korea was the first country placed under an SRF arrangement.

In principle, the pool of currencies at the IMF's disposal exists for the benefit of the entire membership. Each member borrowing another's currency from the pool is therefore expected to return it as soon as its payments problems have been solved. The funds are therefore supposed to revolve through the membership and be available whenever the need arises. Before the IMF releases any money from the pool, the member must therefore demonstrate how it intends to solve its payments problems so that it can repay the IMF within its normal repayment period of three to five years (which in certain cases can be extended up to ten years). In many cases, not only in Africa, but also in Asia, Latin America and Eastern Europe, these repayments periods have proven to be highly unrealistic. The consequence for many poor countries has been a permanent rescheduling and recycling of their IMF loans.

The economic logic behind these requirements is simple: a country with a payments problem is spending more than it is earning and this situation has to stop. Reform is therefore needed. But the country is not free to choose any kind of reform. It has to adopt measures that can be approved by the IMF, because the IMF only lends on the proviso that the member country uses the borrowed money effectively. This means that the borrowing country has to pledge to undertake a series of reforms aimed at eradicating the source of the payments problems. This pledge comes in the form of a reform plan that the potential borrowing country presents to the IMF. In accordance with the neoliberal dogma of the IMF, such reform plans contain the following standard components: reduce government expenditure, tighten monetary policy, and deal with structural weaknesses (for example, privatise inefficient public utilities and enterprises). Lately, due to the IMF's new-found social consciousness, certain other items have been added to this list: adequate social safety nets, 'good' government spending and good governance. It is often highly unclear what these terms mean in practice, but all potential borrowing countries have learnt the importance of including such items in their applications.

The reform programme is supposed to be 'owned' by the country in question rather than the IMF, and the specifics of each IMF-supported adjustment programme determined by the member country. In some cases this is so. For instance, the decisions taken by several authoritarian regimes to tighten social budgets, and maintain or increase military budgets, were not something the IMF argued for or suggested. These were decisions taken by national leaders. That said, all reform plans are evaluated by both IMF staff and the EDs. The final decision rests with the EDs; if they are satisfied, the loan is disbursed in instalments (usually over one to three years) tied to the member's progress in implementing the reform programme. In the many cases where sustained progress is more or less nil, countries seem to stumble into a condition of permanent crisis, from one IMF programme loan to another. In Africa, Kenya is an excellent example of such a country.

There is no such thing as a free lunch, and when a member borrows from the IMF, it pays various charges to cover the IMF's operational expenses and to compensate the member whose currency it is borrowing. The service charge to the IMF is usually around 1 per cent and the interest charge (in recent years) about 4.5 per cent. Both the service charge and the interest charge are slightly below market price, and an IMF member earns interest only on its quota contribution if other members borrow its currency from the pool. For instance, the United Kingdom only earns interest when British pounds are borrowed from the pool, not when US dollars are borrowed. The introduction of the euro opens up the possibility of some interesting bargaining situations between European Union countries.

The United States and the IMF

Concerning the United States and the IMF there are again two competing views. In one interpretation the IMF is the US Treasury's lapdog: it never ventures far without looking back for the approval of its master. This is the popular view outside the US. In the United States, on the other hand, many, for instance in the US Congress, see the role played by the IMF both as costly for the US and as a limitation on US hegemonic power. There is some truth in both of these claims. Words spoken from the US Treasury clearly carry a great deal of weight in the IMF, but the US is not entirely dominant, and the multilateral arrangement that the IMF represents does place some constraints on the US Treasury's ability to act unilaterally in international financial politics.

In theory, there are clear limits to US power. The US controls only 17.16 per cent of the votes. The managing director of the IMF is by convention a European, and Japan (6.16 per cent), Germany (6.02 per cent), France (4.9 per cent) and the United Kingdom (4.97 per cent) could easily outnumber the total number of US votes if these four countries joined together in a coordinated manner. So far this has not happened. In practice, the US is usually able to get the decisions it desires, exercising its influence behind the scenes, often in informal interactions between the first deputy managing director of the IMF (by convention an American) and the deputy secretary of the US Treasury.

In normal times, the US by and large does not get involved, as the EDs discuss, say, the financial budget of Malawi or deregulation of banking in Paraguay. Surveillance is the IMF's main activity, and this is the kind of activity that the US feels comfortable about leaving to the IMF. US power is exercised mainly under two circumstances: first, when the IMF is called upon to rescue a country in deep financial crisis, a situation where the IMF (and the US Treasury) has the leverage to extract commitments in return for financial rescue packages, and second, when strategic American interests are involved. The bail-outs of Russia and South Korea are prime examples of how the US Treasury used its influence over the IMF. The experience with the South Korean rescue packages in December 1997 illustrates the point:

> As South Korea slipped within days of running out of hard currency to pay its debts in December, it sent a secret envoy,

Kim Kihwan, to work out a rescue package. 'I didn't bother going to the IMF,' Mr. Kim recalled recently. 'I called Mr. Summers' office at the Treasury from my home in Seoul, flew to Washington and went directly there. I knew this was how this would be done.' (Sanger 1999: 23)

The agreement was then reached and presented to the IMF and the other multilateral institutions involved as a done deal. The IMF was not very happy about it, but was not in a position to renegotiate the deal struck between the US Treasury and the South Korean government. It had no say over the deal as such, but was left with the task of putting the financial rescue package together. Another institution involved in this package was the ADB, which years later has tried to renegotiate its part of the deal since it leaves the ADB completely overexposed in South Korea.

THE REGIONAL DEVELOPMENT BANKS

Like the World Bank, the regional development banks make loans on near-market terms with funds borrowed from international capital markets. The members of these banks are regional developing countries and donor countries (both regional and non-regional). Although non-regional donor countries as a general rule supply the bulk of the effective capital (meaning the unpaid subscribed capital that constitutes credible guarantees for the funds borrowed in the international capital markets), they do not have majority voting power. However, voting is still weighted in accordance with the capital subscriptions of the member countries represented by the EDs. Here as in the World Bank, countries are organised into country constituencies. In only two cases, Japan and the US, does one country constitute a constituency on its own.

There are quite a number of regional development banks, but here we will only consider the three major ones in the developing world. These are the African Development Bank (AfDB), the Asian Development Bank (ADB) and the Inter-American Development Bank (IDB). Two related factors were central to the creation of the regional development banks. Developing country aspirations, influenced by postcolonial rhetoric about regional cooperation, played a role, but without US geopolitical strategic interests during the Cold War it is doubtful whether these institutions would ever have seen the light of day. The latter factor was especially important for subduing US resistance toward the establishment of the ADB and the IDB.

In Latin America, a regional development bank had been on the agenda for many years, but the establishment of the World Bank gave the United States an excuse to deflect Latin American demands for such a bank until the late 1950s. What tipped the balance in favour of the IDB was the political resentment towards the US in the region,[6] and the revolutionary fever that spread through the region in the aftermath of the Cuban revolution. Once US support was confirmed, an intergovernmental committee, which was established in 1959 to consider the proposal, reached agreement in only three months. By December, the Articles of Agreement were in effect, and the IDB officially began operations in October 1961 (Culpeper 1997). The establishment of the IDB opened the way for regional development banks in Africa and Asia as well.

The argument most widely cited during the process that led to the establishment of the ADB was that additional development funding was needed in Asia. The ADB was not supposed to overlap and duplicate the work of other agencies, but instead focus on potentially viable projects not financed by existing institutions. However, it was also argued that an Asian Bank would be more familiar with Asian needs and demands than an institution with global scope like the World Bank. Similarly, it was argued that an Asian Bank would foster a greater sense of regional cooperation in an area historically beset by strife and poverty.

The question of membership from countries outside the region raised controversies in the process that led to the establishment of the ADB. At some point in the discussions it was suggested by advocates of Asian nationalism that the developing countries of the region should go it alone, even without Japan. The view that prevailed, however, in the careful consensus-building process informally supervised by Japan, was that membership should be as widespread as possible as long as developing Asia had a majority share of the ownership and a majority on the Board. In the end, this issue was resolved by an article in the ADB's Charter, which requires that the regional member states control at least 60 per cent of the total stock of shares. In order to achieve this Australia, Japan and New Zealand are defined as developed, but regional members, and their share of the total stock of capital counts towards the minimum 60 per cent from the region which is necessary according to the Charter. In donor/borrowing-country terms, the developing-country Asia bloc would therefore be in a minority of only 45 per cent if the developed regional member countries were to vote, so to speak, the other way. In practice, the ADB, like most other MDBs, does not often resort to the casting of votes. Decision making by consensus is the rule; but just as in the World Bank, it is important that the consensus that emerges from the Board meetings reflects the voting power of member countries. Nevertheless, due to the specific political contexts of the regional development banks, the power structures of these institutions do not depend merely on contributions and votes. Issues concerning regional identity are also an important part of the picture. The role of Japan in the ADB underlines this point. Japan is both a donor and a regional member country. This places it in a dual position in between regional borrowing countries and non-regional donor countries.

The AfDB is the only MDB originally established without external donor countries. The argument was that the admission of non-regional members would create problems of governance, leadership and ownership, and also threaten the newly gained independence of the African countries. Thus, at the inaugural meeting of the Organisation of African Unity (OAU) in May 1963, it was decided that the AfDB should be an African institution financed with African capital and run by the Africans themselves. This freedom from external pressure came at a high price. The AfDB was constantly short of funds. It soon proved extremely difficult to raise the resources needed on international capital markets based only on African subscriptions. This debate started in the early 1970s, but it was not resolved until the AfDB's annual meeting in Lusaka in May 1982, when non-regional members were incorporated. This clearly added a new dimension of regional identity to the politics of the AfDB. It did what all the rhetoric about 'African unity' had not managed: it glued the regional member countries together. Suddenly it became 'us' vs. 'them'. The regional countries controlled about 66 per cent of the votes on the Board of Directors, and the new non-regional members about 34 per cent. In the soft-window facility of the AfDB the votes are split 50–50 between regional and non-regional countries.

Whereas the two other regional development banks that we are concerned with here – the ADB and IDB – today are perceived as financially solid and mature development institutions, the AfDB is the exception. Throughout the 1980s and 1990s this institution was haunted by increased political conflict about management and control over the Bank. The most powerful African country in the AfDB, Nigeria, increasingly felt that its supremacy over the institution was threatened by a conspiracy by the non-regional countries. The outcome of this struggle was that the AfDB got its credit rating reduced from AAA to AA in 1995, the only major MDB to do so. In 2002, the AfDB is only just starting to recover from the controversies and political conflicts of the 1990s.

THE UNITED NATIONS DEVELOPMENT PROGRAMME

The establishment of the United Nations Development Program (UNDP) in 1965 was based on the amalgamation of several UN agencies. In contrast to the MDBs, the UNDP does not have a specific mandate formulated in articles of agreement or a charter. Formally, UNDP is supervised by the UN's Economic and Social Council (ECOSOC), but in practice it operates quite independently. The activities of the UNDP are coordinated from its headquarters in New York.

When UNDP was established, the UN's General Assembly placed effective authority over UNDP policy in the hands of an Executive Board.[7] This Board has 36 members, appointed in accordance with the following regional framework: 8 members from Africa, 7 from Asia, 5 from Latin America and the Caribbean, 4 from Eastern Europe and 12 from Western Europe and North America. Voting power in the UNDP is not determined by a member's financial contribution as in the MDBs. Similar to the general procedure of the UN, the executive board members have voting power on a one country, one vote basis. Decisions are by simple majority. This means that the developing countries have a majority in the cases in which votes are cast at the Board. Thus, in theory, the developing countries have much more power here than in many other agencies in the multilateral system. But consensus and not voting is the rule also in the UNDP. According to the UNDP (1997: 8) itself,[8] 'the practice of striving for consensus in decision-making shall be encouraged'. However, it is widely acknowledged that the major donors have great influence in the UNDP: they pick up the bill, and therefore it is their wishes that often prevail (see Kalderén 1991; Klingebiel 1999; Dam 2002). The Executive Board works through a number of committees and meets twice a year. The Board also reports to ECOSOC and the General Assembly.

The Executive Board formulates the general policy of the UNDP, sets priorities and reviews and approves programmes, activities and the budget. The Executive Board is known in the UNDP as the 'policy filter'. This means that the Board has the opportunity to veto a policy line. However, of equal importance is the role of the Board as a meeting place where consensus between developed and developing countries can be constructed. The Board is therefore important both for the UNDP's internal and external legitimacy (Dam 2002).

The head of the UNDP is known as the Administrator. The person for this position is selected by the UN Secretary General and later confirmed by the General Assembly. The Administrator is the top executive of the UNDP's secretariat and its programmes. It is worth noting that the head of the UNDP's Human Development Report Office (HDRO) has also the status of special adviser to the Administrator. This creates a strong and continuous link between the Administrator and the UNDP's external flagship document.

Another important feature with the UNDP is the Resident Representatives. These are found in more than 130 countries around the world, making the UNDP one of the very few multilateral institutions with staff in almost all developing countries. Even the World Bank cannot compete with the country-wide reach of the UNDP.

Financing the UNDP

Unlike the MDBs, the UNDP does not lend money to developing countries, but gives technical assistance through grants. The UNDP is therefore constantly in need of funding. The UNDP is mainly financed on a voluntary basis by member states. Their contributions can be divided into core and non-core resources. Core resources are spent in accordance with priorities set by the UNDP through its ordinary programmes, whereas non-core resources (trust funds, etc.) are subject to conditions and restrictions imposed by the donor countries. One major challenge for the UNDP is that its proportion of core resources available has fallen significantly during the last two decades.[9]

During its history, the UNDP has faced several serious financial crises. Compared with other multilateral institutions, its financial capacity and potential is clearly limited (Klingebiel 1999). By comparison, the World Bank has, since the early 1980s, spent far more resources on technical assistance than the UNDP. The World Bank is in fact 13 times larger than the UNDP in financial terms. In 2001 the total financial disbursement of the World Bank was US$17,251 million, whereas the comparable figure in the UNDP was US$1,300 million. This discrepancy led the Nordic UN Project to conclude already in 1990 that 'UNDP has not been able to attract sufficient resources to play the central funding and co-ordinating role foreseen' (Edgren and Möller 1991: 154).

In order to try to achieve some level of long-term perspective in its planning, the UNDP organises special donor meetings, so-called 'pledging conferences'. These conferences give the UNDP some idea of the kind of financial commitment the institution can expect from its donor countries over a period of more than one year, but no guarantees are provided. The UNDP therefore has a broad base of potential donors, but it lacks a firm financial base. The system of voluntary contributions also makes the UNDP dependent on a relatively small group of countries (Klingebiel 1999). In the 1990s, the so-called 'like-minded countries' (the Nordic countries, The Netherlands and Canada) emerged as the most important donor country group for the UNDP. The general decrease in official development assistance (ODA) has made the UNDP increasingly dependent on this small group of countries. It was therefore a major blow financially for the UNDP when Denmark significantly reduced its contributions to the UNDP in 1999 (after Mark Malloch Brown was selected as Administrator over the Danish candidate). This means that the UNDP during the 1990s increasingly found itself facing a stark choice: to continue in its attempt to be the major provider and coordinator of technical assistance, or to transform itself to an upstream policy adviser. The UNDP under Mark Malloch Brown chose the latter option, and focused on governance and governance-related issues (see Chapters 3 and 4). This choice was largely by default: the UNDP has never been given the resources needed to fulfil its mandate as the coordinator of technical assistance.

THE WORLD TRADE ORGANISATION

The WTO was established on 1 January 1995, as part of the final agreements of the Uruguay Round negotiations. The establishment of the WTO is one of the most significant events in the recent history of multilateral institutions, because 'its establishment provides a sister institution for the Bretton Woods pairing of the International Monetary Fund (IMF) and the World Bank some 50 years after their creation' (O'Brien et al. 2000: 68). The roots of the WTO, however, can be traced back to December 1945 when the United States invited 14 countries to begin negotiations on liberalising world trade. The negotiations had two objectives: to create an International Trade Organisation (ITO) that would facilitate trading relations as the World Bank and the IMF facilitated monetary relations, and to implement as soon as possible an agreement to reduce tariff levels. The second exercise resulted in the General Agreement on Tariffs and Trade (GATT), which was signed on 30 October 1947. The idea was that once the ITO was established, GATT would be subsumed in the larger organisation. However, the US Congress refused to give its agreement to the ITO. In fact, congressional opinion against the ITO was so strong that in December 1950 the US administration dropped the initiative and asked Congress to continue giving its support to GATT.

Like its predecessor, GATT, the WTO is not a multilateral development institution, but a multilateral trading institution. Its main purpose is to organise multilateral trade negotiations to reduce tariffs and nontariff barriers (NTBs) to trade. From its predecessor, WTO also inherited a neoliberal paradigm, a technical approach to trade and a tradition of secrecy and lack of transparency (Bøås and Vevatne 2003). Of all the multilateral institutions we are concerned with in this book, the WTO is the one that is least open to public control and civil society participation. This has made it possible for staff members to isolate themselves from new impulses and competing worldviews and perspectives. The events in Seattle in 1999 were a huge shock for most WTO staff members.

The creation of the WTO can be seen as a conscious attempt to establish a strong global regulatory framework in support of increased trade liberalisation. The architects of the post-Second World War economic order interpreted international non-cooperation on trade as a function of domestic pressures. GATT was therefore set up as a government-to-government contract anchored in support for freer trade (Esty 1994). By embedding the principles of liberal trade theory in an international regime, the individuals and governments behind the creation of GATT not only built an institutional mechanism for the supposed reduction of trade conflict among member states, they also heightened their commitment to liberal trade theory to almost a constitutional level. The consequence was a clear limitation on the power of governments to accede to the special pleadings of various national interest groups and other social movements. In moving free trade principles to a higher place of authority, a buffer was constructed not only against protectionist pressures, but also against most other attempts at reform of the international trade regime.

One approach to the WTO is therefore to view it not only as a legal instrument for the promotion of free trade and the combating of protectionism (O'Brien et al. 2000), but also as a bastion of a certain (neoliberal) worldview of economic activity in general. According to the WTO, free trade and the abolishment of all kinds of trade barriers will promote economic growth, not only among the rich industrial countries, but worldwide. Trade liberalisation will encourage more efficient use of resources, the adoption and diffusion of cleaner technologies, higher productivity and increased income levels. The prime assumption of the WTO is therefore that trade liberalisation will enable a higher number of less developed countries to tackle the problem of poverty, as well as other problems, such as widespread environmental degradation. The law of comparative advantage and the superiority of market-based solutions are articles of faith in the WTO.

The WTO, development and power

In the WTO, the major events are Ministerial Meetings, which often lead to multilateral rounds of trade negotiations. Among the most famous ones are the Tokyo Round and the Uruguay Round. The Seattle meeting also contributed to WTO fame, if not glory (we will return to the implications from Seattle in Chapter 4, when we discuss what we call the 'politics of protest'). The WTO Ministerial Meeting that followed after Seattle took place in Doha, Qatar. The new round of trade negotiations that this meeting was supposed to start has been defined by the WTO as a Development Round.

The Seattle meeting in November 1999 was held against a background of massive protests from thousands of people from lobby groups and NGOs. Developing countries walked out in protest when the United States threatened to link trade with labour standards. The leaders of many poor countries saw this as a scheme to bar their goods from Western markets. In Seattle many developing countries had been ill prepared for the negotiations. When they arrived at Doha, however, most of them had done their homework. They also found it very disturbing and provocative that the negotiating text of what was defined as the Development Round had been drafted in Geneva without their participation. What they experienced in Doha was even more arm-twisting.

According to several observers,[10] immense pressure was exerted on the poorer countries by the powerful trading nations who threatened to withdraw aid and debt relief, among other things, in order to get their way. At one point, two countries – one from Latin America, the other from Africa – were threatened with the removal of agreed access to richer country markets. And Uganda was even asked by a senior US official to remove its ambassador to the WTO from Geneva because he disagreed with the US on key policy areas.

The political game that was played out in Doha was very far from being a development round. Rather it was an illustrative example of what in America is called 'hard ball': every strategic weakness in the opposition, this time the majority of developing countries, was seized upon and taken advantage of. The WTO is therefore very different from the other multilateral institutions we are concerned with in this book. The veil of multilateralism and consensus is much thinner in the WTO than in the MDBs, the IMF and the UNDP, and the neoliberal paradigm is much more vividly present. The exercise of power is therefore also less hidden. The kind of blatant arm-twisting that took place in Doha is not something we would expect to see at an annual World Bank or ADB meeting.

THE ROLES AND APPROACHES OF MULTILATERAL INSTITUTIONS: THE DOCTRINE OF POLITICAL NEUTRALITY

Almost all multilateral institutions are defined in their agreements and charters as functional and technical institutions.[11] The legitimacy of the World Bank and the other multilateral institutions rests on the assumption that their development advice reflects the best possible technical research, a justification readily cited by borrowing governments.[12] All aspects of the activities of multilateral institutions are however highly political. Whether it comes in the form of technical assistance, programme lending or policy advice, these activities involve hard political questions and choices. The strategy applied by the multilateral institutions in order to remain within their functional and technical charters can best be understood as one of 'depoliticisation', defined as 'the process of placing at one remove the political character of decision-making' (Burnham 2001: 127). This technocratic form of governance is one that multilateral institutions have practised ever since they came into being. Thus, the Charters of respectively the African Development Bank and the Asian Development Bank specify that:

> The Bank shall not accept loans or assistance that could in any way prejudice, limit, deflect or otherwise alter its purpose or functions. The Bank, its President, Vice presidents, officers and staff shall not interfere in the political affairs of any member; not shall they be influenced in their decisions by the political character of the member country concerned. Only economic considerations shall be relevant to their decisions. (AfDB 1964: art. 38; ADB 1966: art. 36)

Similarly, in the Articles of Agreement of the World Bank it is stated that:

> The Bank and its officers shall not interfere in the political affairs of any member country; nor shall they be influenced in their decisions by the political character of the member or members concerned. Only economic considerations shall be relevant to their decisions, and these considerations shall be weighted impartially in order to achieve the purposes stated in Article 1. (World Bank 1989: art. IV, section 10)

This is of course true only on a rhetorical level. Political considerations have always been an integrated part of decision making in multilateral institutions, and likewise all decisions taken by these institutions have political implications for their member countries. However, by applying this strategy of depoliticisation it became possible for multilateral institutions to retain, in many instances, arm's-length control over crucial economic and social processes, whilst simultaneously benefiting from the distancing effects of depoliticisation. Decisions are taken, not in the name of an ideology or from the vantage point of certain specific political interests, but in the name of rationality and for the greater common good. Policies are cloaked in a technocratic and functional language, and ideas and approaches that appear too political for multilateral institutions are drained of political content through rhetorical processes. This doctrine of neutrality and technicality has defined the three dominant roles of multilateral institutions: as providers of technical and financial assistance, and as suppliers of policy advice.

The three roles of multilateral institutions: technical assistance, programme lending and policy advice

These three roles are important for almost all multilateral institutions (the only major exception is the WTO). Loans and technical assistance for projects was the first role that these institutions assumed, and throughout their existence this has been an important aspect of their work. However, over time the roles, activities and lending programmes of multilateral institutions have been broadened considerably. The changing scope of the role of the World Bank is illustrative of this process.

Assistance through project lending is still of extreme importance for the World Bank and its client countries. However, the narrow project focus in the World Bank was challenged quite early. The structure of lending clearly had changed already during Robert McNamara's presidency (that is, 1968–81). Project lending still dominated the World Bank's portfolio, but gradually more resources were channelled into programme lending. McNamara's vision was to transform the World Bank from being a bank for infrastructure projects to a development agency. Many observers and critics of the World Bank will say that this transformation has never been achieved, but most would agree that the process of transformation that started in the World Bank has later been initiated in the other major multilateral institutions.

The structural adjustment programmes (SAPs) implemented first in Sub-Saharan Africa and later elsewhere in Asian and Latin American countries are perhaps the best example of programme lending from multilateral institutions, but it is also important to be aware that programme lending from these institutions has taken many forms, and there are considerable differences in approaches both within institutions (between different types of programme loans) and between multilateral institutions (for instance, between the World Bank's programme loans and those of the regional development banks). Most often the conditionalities attached to programme loans from regional development banks are more flexible than those of the World Bank.

One important aspect of the broadening of the agenda of the World Bank and other multilateral institutions was that it implied new challenges with respect to competence and understanding of complex societal processes. More emphasis was therefore placed on economic and social research. In particular, this has been evident in the World Bank. Research has helped to legitimise an increasingly prominent role for the World Bank in policy analysis and advice. Being a highly centralised agency, the task of building an efficient and coherent research unit was quite easy in the World Bank. Due to the high priority given to economic research by every World Bank president since Robert McNamara, this unit has grown into a hegemonic interpreter of the economics of development. World Bank research is less famous for the creation of new ideas than for adopting, adapting – and even distorting – ideas; its ability to disseminate and translate academic ideas into operational policy advice has made the World Bank a world authority on development. The World Bank's resources for development economics research are larger than those of any university or research institution. The size of the research budget, the number of economists employed and the leverage it gains not only from its lending operations but also from its most important member countries are indicative of the hegemonic position that the World Bank enjoys in the production of a certain type of knowledge about development. In the 1980s and 1990s, this knowledge fell within the neoliberal economic paradigm. An important manifestation of the World Bank's position is the *World Development Report* (*WDR*). This annual publication series was initiated by McNamara in 1978. Its current worldwide circulation is approximately 120,000 copies. The only other similar publication that can match this is the *Human Development Report* (*HDR*) of the UNDP. The *HDR* was first published in 1990. The directness of its challenge to existing orthodoxy, the coherent presentation of the case for human development and its style quickly established a niche for the *HDR* in the global development debate that was partly in opposition to the views of the World Bank.

Over time, policy advice moved up the ladder of importance in most multilateral institutions. In particular, good governance became the new buzzword of multilateral institutions during the 1990s. The World Bank and the regional development banks were important actors within this debate, whereas the IMF and the WTO adapted much more slowly to the new situation. However, the multilateral institution which went furthest in this direction was the UNDP under Mark Malloch Brown, which – albeit partly by default – started to transform itself from a provider of technical assistance to an upstream policy adviser on good governance. This raises the question of the relationship between the key multilateral institutions, which may be briefly addressed before we, in the following chapter, go more deeply into the historical evolution of multilateral development policies.

THE RELATIONSHIP BETWEEN MULTILATERAL INSTITUTIONS

The relationship between multilateral institutions is ambiguous. The institutions that make up the multilateral system are both collaborators and competitors, and the balance between these two aspects of their interaction changes over time. Most would argue that the World Bank is the unquestionable leader, and that the other multilateral institutions tend to follow World Bank policies and approaches. This view is too simplistic. There is much more to the dynamics of the multilateral system than 'follow the leader'. Each multilateral institution has its own agenda that it will try to achieve. This is necessary both for its legitimacy and future funding.

The World Bank has its own agenda, developed in whatever niche its president can identify between its various constituencies, of which the most influential ones are the US Treasury and (more recently) the community of international NGOs based in Washington DC. The World Bank, paradoxically, is both a bastion of neoliberalism and a quite progressive development institution concerned with local participation and needs. The regional development banks, in particular the ADB and IDB, try to define their own development agendas based on what is perceived as the uniqueness of their respective regions' developmental experience. On several important issues they take views that are slightly in opposition to those articulated by the World Bank.[13] With the region as their main referent, the regional development banks most often adopt new mandates and modalities by negotiating a regional consensus, after a policy is formally adopted at the World Bank. A major exception to this pattern is the ADB on the issue of governance. In fact, whereas many assume that the regional development banks fit a common pattern and are satellites commanded from a World Bank centre, they have differing origins and histories, and differing relations regarding the World Bank, which create a recipe for a somewhat competitive pluralism among the MDBs.

The relationship between the World Bank and the UNDP is highly competitive, and especially since the World Bank started to turn itself into a development agency. Both with respect to finances and staff numbers, the World Bank is a giant compared to the UNDP. The latter was supposed to be the agency for general aid coordination in all less developed countries. But this is a position the UNDP has never been able to claim, mainly due to lack of sufficient resources. The only organisation which has had this kind of funding is the World Bank, and as it slowly moved in on what used to be UNDP prime territory, the relationship between these two institutions became increasingly competitive. The publication of the *World Development Report* and the *Human Development Report* should be interpreted in this regard. And it is World Bank dominance within technical assistance, programme lending and issues concerning aid coordination that has led to the recent reconsideration of UNDP activity, moving away from technical assistance and into policy advice. Bluntly speaking, we can define this as a strategy of default. It is much cheaper to give policy advice than to provide technical assistance. It remains to be seen how much leverage over policy this advice will have in practice, if the UNDP lacks the necessary resources to make their advice 'palatable'.

The IMF and the WTO are, at least so far, much less engaged in strategic games of collaboration and competition. However, as these institutions increasingly become involved in development issues, they will have to start developing institutional 'foreign policies' towards the other actors that inhabit the multilateral system.

CONCLUDING REMARKS

The organisation and financing of multilateral institutions is a complex matter, and to outsiders their systems may seem opaque. This is exacerbated by the fact that a special language has been developed around these activities which make them even less transparent. This is one reason why many staff members of multilateral institutions feel that criticism directed towards them is often unfair. The fault may, however, lie not so much in the ignorance of civil society, but rather the democratic deficit that exists in the multilateral system. The political and economic system in and around multilateral institutions has become so complex that it is nearly impossible for even a highly informed public opinion to penetrate it. This sort of exclusion (whether deliberate or not) creates frustration which may lead either to apathy or protest. We do not oppose the latter response, indeed we support it, but we do think that protest – no matter how critical – should be based on an informed opinion on what multilateral institutions actually are and what is going on within them. In this chapter we have tried to highlight what we see as the most important features of the major institutions of the multilateral system. It is an understanding of these features that should, in our view, underpin the response of civil society to multilateral institutions – in the spirit of 'critical engagement'.

3
The Changing Priorities of Multilateral Institutions: From Technical Aid to Good Governance

In this chapter we will describe how the agendas of multilateral institutions have developed over time. At face value it may seem that they have changed considerably: from technical aid to good governance. But the implicit knowledge which has underpinned these agendas has been within a single, and rather unchanging, frame of reference. The agenda of these institutions has been broadened, but this process has taken place within established and largely unquestioned boundaries, firmly kept in place by a certain frame of knowledge. As in the heyday of technical assistance, knowledge is still mainly understood in instrumental terms: as a non-political and objective tool that, if correctly implemented, will lead to better policies. Such an attitude to knowledge creates a strong dichotomy between that which is within the frame (relevant) or outside it (irrelevant) (see Bøås and McNeill 2003).

From the end of the 1980s, the agenda in multilateral institutions expanded well beyond narrowly technical questions of project choice and design, to address broader issues such as sustainable development, good governance, and participatory approaches to development, gender, and indigenous peoples. But the broadening of the agenda has taken place firmly within the old mode of thinking, of modernisation and economic growth, associated with a knowledge frame of a technical and functional approach to development. Knowledge is still viewed in very 'instrumental' and apolitical terms:

> The current concern with 'good governance' and 'best practice' provides a good example of the instrumentalisation of development knowledge: what appears as knowledge is shaped by the need to intervene. The appeal of such concepts lies in their apparent instrumentality: if one can identify problems in Third World states as resulting from bad or inefficient practices of

governance, the solution would seem to be to reform these practices. (Nustad and Sending 2000: 55)

It is this kind of mindset that led the World Bank to interpret the African crisis as a crisis of governance (defined in technocratic terms) in the late 1980s. We will return to this issue later in this chapter, but here it suffices to say that the new policies adopted have so far not led multilateral institutions into a deeply reflective mood that would entail a real re-examination of means and ends. To a considerable degree they still operate under old standard operating procedures and organisational routines. Development (and the lack of it) is still mainly addressed as a technical issue. The aim in this chapter is therefore to analyse not only to what extent the approach of multilateral institutions has changed, or remained, but also why this is so. It is also apparent that the situation is not the same in all multilateral institutions, with regard to different issue-areas. To highlight the differences between the institutions under study, we will first consider the World Bank, then our three regional development banks, and finally the IMF and the WTO.[1] Finally, this chapter will consider policy changes across the spectrum of multilateral institutions, and what kind of challenges the new good governance agenda poses for the established frame of knowledge in multilateral institutions.

IN THE BEGINNING ... MODERNISATION THROUGH TECHNICAL ASSISTANCE

The idea of 'development' can be traced far back in time (see Sachs 1995; Escobar 1995; Nustad 2003), but it is in the post-war period that the idea of development is made explicit. Truman's inaugural presidential address in 1949 can be seen as the starting point for the development project (see Chapter 1). According to Escobar (1995), Truman's speech captures its essence: the Third World (as it came to be known in both development theory and in the language of multilateral institutions) is backward and primitive, but one day their problems will be solved, and the solution will come through these countries following the same path to wealth and prosperity as the civilised Western world. Although different economic strategies – notably Keynesianism and neoliberalism – have been employed over the years to promote development, the overall goal has been the same: bringing the so-called Third World countries and societies more in line with our own. In the early days of development the achievement of this transition was sought through the provision of assistance for infrastructure projects, whereas today the emphasis is more on 'macro' policies: good governance in the form of a market economy and Western-style multi-party democracy.

The goal has always been modernisation, and development was promoted by the World Bank as an explicit alternative to communism (Nustad 2003), 'the false philosophy which has made such headway throughout the world, misleading many peoples and adding to their sorrows and their difficulties' (Caufield 1996: 48). The World Bank began its operations with a narrow focus on assistance for infrastructure development. The development project promoted by multilateral institutions was never politically neutral, but underdevelopment was explained in terms of obstacles, internal to the countries concerned, ideologically neutral and solvable by technical, pragmatic means (Gardner and Lewis 1996).

The World Bank: from the beginning to the establishment of the International Development Association

At the outset, post-war reconstruction was considered to be the main area of business for the World Bank, as indicated by the title – the International Bank for Reconstruction and Development (which is now the name of its 'hard window'). Thus, six of the nine loan applications received by the end of April 1947 were for European reconstruction, in Czechoslovakia, Denmark, France, Luxemburg, The Netherlands and Poland (Bergesen and Lunde 1999).

The period of economic reconstruction was also one of major political change, and the post-war world was faced with a choice between two ways of life: communism and democracy. In 1947, the United Kingdom withdrew its troops from the civil war raging in Greece, an act that led to the Truman Doctrine, which had important implications for the World Bank. In the face of what was perceived as a dangerous increase in support for communist parties in Europe, the Truman administration argued that a speedy European recovery required levels of assistance that far exceeded the capacity of the World Bank. This effort therefore had to be financed by American taxpayers through a bilateral economic recovery programme. Such a programme was first proposed in public by the Secretary of State George Marshall. The initiation of the Marshall Plan made it possible for the World Bank to turn its attention to the long-term problems of less developed countries, beginning with Latin America.

The World Bank, however, was at this stage ill-prepared to assume a major role in development financing. Its financial resources were small and many of the world's poorest countries could not afford its near-market interest rates. An International Finance Corporation (IFC) and an International Development Association (IDA) linked to the World Bank were proposed in 1951 by a US advisory group appointed by the Truman administration to recommend ways to achieve the goals set out in his inaugural speech. The objective of this group was not only to suggest ways to facilitate development in general, but more precisely to suggest ways in which to strengthen key countries in the Third World, that is those surrounding the emerging Soviet bloc, and to discourage them from seeking alignment with the Soviet Union (Gwin 1994). Using aid for strategic geopolitical purposes was to become a hallmark for much multilateral development funding during the Cold War, and many autocrats in Africa and elsewhere became adept at this game. An extreme example was President Mobutu in Zaire, who allied himself firmly with the Western camp, but also let it be known informally that this could change if funding from multilateral institutions were reduced. Mobutu and his peers in other Third World countries managed to redirect huge amounts of foreign aid into their Swiss bank accounts.

In its recommendations, the advisory group recommended the establishment of some form of multilateral arrangement for providing finance on terms somewhere between loans and grants. The group proposed that the United States should take the lead in establishing both an IFC and an IDA affiliated with the World Bank: the IFC to mobilise capital for direct lending to the private sector and IDA to provide concessional loans to poor countries using funds contributed by governments. In the early 1950s, the response by the US government to these suggestions was only lukewarm. The United States was at war in Korea, facing a growing budget deficit, and still not entirely convinced that more resources really were needed for developing countries, despite pressure from Third World countries within the UN for larger amounts of development funding on softer terms. The pressure from developing countries was increasing, for three main reasons:

1. the number of countries belonging to this group was rapidly increasing due to decolonialisation;
2. the inability of many of these countries to afford ordinary World Bank loans;
3. the perception of enormous amounts of aid having been given to Europe through the Marshall Plan.

The consequence was that these countries started to use the UN system, arguing in discussions for the establishment of a new UN development agency that would provide technical and financial assistance on concessional terms (it was these discussions which also led to the establishment of the UNDP in 1965). This new UN development agency, they argued, should operate under the UN system of one country, one vote, instead of the World Bank system of weighted voting. Not surprisingly, the United States, and also most Western European countries, strongly opposed this.

However, in this debate, Cold War strategies played an influential role. Concerned with Soviet attempts to exploit the UN debate on financing for development, the US State Department realised that some response had to be made from their side. The US government therefore first searched for an inexpensive gesture: the IFC proposal. This proposal was in 1954 presented to both the US Congress and House of Representatives as a contribution to prosperity, increased trade, and the peace and solidarity of the free world (Sanford 1982). The proposal passed through with wide support and little debate.

The establishment of the IFC was, however, not enough to stop demands for a new concessional aid agency in the UN. These demands continued with equal strength until a member of the US Congress took an independent initiative in 1958. The favourable response to this individual proposal, combined with even more pressure from the developing countries for a Special UN Fund for Economic Development (SUNFED) and the fact that many developing countries rapidly were reaching the limits of their creditworthiness in the World Bank, convinced the government of the United States to start consultations with the World Bank's president about presenting to the World Bank's Board a plan for an IDA. The outcome of this process was that the IDA was established in 1960. And, as had been recommended by Truman's advisory board ten years earlier, the United States took a major share (42 per cent) in the first round of IDA contributions. With the establishment of the IDA, the first phase of the history of what now came to be known as the World Bank was complete.[2] Having played an important, but also reluctant, part in this process, the United States now encouraged the World Bank to expand its lending to low-income countries, and in particular to become more involved in addressing the need for increased agricultural productivity. Huge projects were carried out to meet this need, most involving the construction of irrigation works, dams and roads. Through financial and technical assistance for infrastructure, the world was to be saved from hunger and poverty.

The period of project assistance 1945–80

From the late 1940s to the early 1960s, development assistance was mainly bilateral. However, from the mid-1960s to the mid-1970s, through the creation of the regional development banks and the UNDP as well as a range of other UN agencies and smaller regional and sub-regional arrangements, a major expansion in multilateral aid took place.

For over three decades development assistance focused primarily on investment projects in infrastructure, agriculture, industry and (later) the social sectors. The multilateral institutions in particular were perceived as the world's leading specialists in the planning, supervising, monitoring and executing of project-based investments (IDS 2000).

The main objective was to accelerate economic growth in developing countries. More precisely a target was set of increasing national income of developing countries by 5 per cent per annum by 1970 (Legum 1970). With population growth at an estimated rate of 2.5 per cent per annum, this was taken to be sufficient to double living standards in 20 to 30 years. Quantitative targets for agriculture and industry were set and broad goals also established for agriculture, natural resources, water, mineral resources and energy, for small-scale industrial development, for health and housing, transport and communications (Emmerij, Jolly and Weiss 2001).

The question at this time was not what to do, but only how to do it. Leading thinkers of this age were deeply influenced by the

Keynesian paradigm of an active interventionist macroeconomic full employment policy as well as the experiences of Roosevelt's New Deal and the creation of a national welfare system in the United Kingdom after the end of the Second World War. It was generally assumed that such successes and precedents were transferable to developing countries as well.

The state was the central feature of these conceptualisations of development. National development plans were the key to modernisation (as they were also in the Soviet Union and other communist countries). Through such plans, the state was supposed to create an investment pool by mobilising domestic and foreign resources. The 'two-gap' model (lack of savings and lack of foreign exchange) exerted considerable influence in both theory and practice. National development plans commonly used the economists' (Harrod-Domar) model to calculate what rate of saving, supplemented by foreign aid, was necessary to achieve the target rate of economic growth. The investment thus financed was to be directed largely to industrial expansion. New industries were to be allowed some protection through import-substitution strategies supported by appropriate tariff and quota policies. Development was thus understood to be equivalent to growth in per capita GNP (gross national product), and the fate of humanity was defined as a common progression: linear, convergent, predictable and manageable. This view also divided the world sharply along a North–South divide. The less developed countries were defined as what the developed world was not; but they too would eventually become like the rich North. Modernisation was therefore the unquestioned and attainable goal, to be achieved by following the proven success of the industrial states, adopting their economic models and technology. It was also generally assumed that the road to modernity would not be a long one, because late-comers would catch up quickly through transfer of knowledge and technology from rich to poor. This was the golden age of technical assistance. It was within this intellectual climate that the UN declared the 1960s to be the decade of development. During a ten-year period, it was claimed, the backwardness of developing countries would be overcome. They would have moved along the continuum to industrialisation and modernity. Rostow's *Stages of Growth* (sub-title *A Non-communist Manifesto*) was highly influential in establishing the conventional wisdom. As the historian

Hobsbawm put it: 'whatever the conscious or unconscious objectives of those who shaped the history of the backward world, modernization, that is to say, the imitation of Western-derived models, was the necessary and indispensable way to achieve them' (Hobsbawm 1994: 203).

Faith in this possibility was sustained by the economic success of this age. From the late 1940s to the early 1970s the world economy grew at an unprecedented rate. Supported by the Marshall Plan, the European countries recovered and grew at nearly 5 per cent per year. Led by Japan, the economies of Asia registered average growth rates of 6 per cent. Brazil doubled its per capita output in an 18-year period, and Latin America as a whole experienced annual growth of 5.3 per cent. Africa also grew rapidly in this period at 4.4 per cent. The two decades from 1950 to 1970 were a period of unparalleled economic growth. The multilateral institutions may be credited for some of this growth, but with hindsight it is clear that little attention was paid to the distribution of the benefits that resulted. Increased income can be used for wise investment in the future or for short-term consumption by political and economic elites. The 'golden age' of development was also the golden age of economic growth as the single measurement of development, and questions of distribution were largely absent from the development debate in multilateral institutions in the 1960s.

In the 1970s, this situation changed as economies in the North first 'overheated' and then went into recession. Very rapid growth in the Organisation for Economic Cooperation and Development (OECD) countries (7.5 per cent in the twelve months from July 1972) was followed by a real fall in GDP (gross domestic product) for the first time since the war: 'The world economy did not recover its old stride after the crash. An era was at an end. The decades since 1973 were to become once again an age of crisis' (Hobsbawm 1994: 286). The oil crisis of 1973, leading to a dramatic increase in the oil price, marked a major turning-point, both in the world economy and in North–South relations. It was only one of several factors that led the major economies into a period of inflation, recession and unemployment; but it also substantially changed the power of – at least a few – countries in the South:

For the first time a group of countries outside the circle of the industrialized world was able to exert its own powerful economic pressure ... This gave the whole North–South dialogue a new impetus, though it still did not produce great progress in the 1970s. As the decade drew to a close, the world economy was in serious difficulties and the institutional framework which had served it since the war was inadequate to resolve them. (Brandt 1980: 41)

The buoyant optimism regarding modernisation and universal development was being challenged, and the earlier consensus on the inevitability of progress through state-led capitalism and national planning was under attack both from the left and the right.

On the left, radical theories of underdevelopment perceived the world economy as a system in which developing countries were poor at least in part because the developed countries were rich, thus challenging whether it was possible for the South ever to 'catch up'. Such analyses ranged from an extreme version, in which underdevelopment was seen as a process imposed on the South by the North, to the observation that the terms of trade for countries exporting primary products were steadily declining.

On the right, some were inspired by the arguments of Peter Bauer's *Dissent on Development* from 1972. In this book Bauer argued that the foundations of current development theory were not only intellectually flawed, but that they also led to policies that were entirely anti-development.[3] Inspired by Bauer's book, neoliberal economists such as Anne Krueger and Harry Johnson started to argue that the state-led development approaches of Keynesianism were discouraging for individual entrepreneurship and private enterprises and encouraged rent-seeking behaviour.

The middle ground is well represented by the publication *Redistribution with Growth* written by a group of economists from the World Bank and the Institute of Development Studies in Britain. It is significant that the book starts with an uncompromising summary of experience by its author, Hollis Chenery, then head of the World Bank Research department (and co-author, with Strout, of one of the most influential articles in development economics (Chenery and Strout 1966)): 'It is now clear that more than a decade of rapid growth in under-developed countries has been of little or no benefit to perhaps a third of their population' (Chenery 1974: xiii). But the prescription seemed reformist and technocratic rather than radical. The concept of 'redistribution with growth' was based on the optimistic assumption that growth would be sufficient to ensure that redistribution could occur without anyone's income falling. And it was suggested that governments might give more weight to benefits that accrued to the poorer members of their population. (This was the heyday of cost-benefit analysis: a technical economic procedure for assessing the benefits and costs of proposed investment projects which was designed to take account of 'distortions' in the economies of developing countries – notably with regard to foreign exchange rates and hidden unemployment.)

The countries of the South demanded a 'New International Economic Order', seeking to assert the power they felt they had gained. The reformist model focused on policies within developing countries, and urged the adoption of 'basic needs' strategies and intermediate (labour-intensive) technologies. This was challenged by many developing countries as an attempt to hold them back technologically.[4] The 1970s therefore started as a decade in which radical changes in the balance of economic power and the international order seemed likely to occur. But the outcome was rather different than anticipated. There was a sharp reduction of economic growth rates in the wake of the oil crisis. The slowdown was most clearly present in Eastern Europe and Africa, where average rates of growth became negative, and in Latin America, where the rate of economic growth barely exceeded that of the population increase. Although 1973 is a useful marker for the end of the golden years, the process of transition began before this and took some time to play out. This applies not only to economic growth but also to development assistance. The level of official development assistance stagnated at the end of the 1960s, leading to 'increasing dissatisfaction and sensitiveness of the developing countries, fully matching the aid weariness of some of the donors' (Pearson 1969: 77):

> It is precisely because the developing countries see their forward momentum threatened by bleak aid prospects that they feel a growing sense of frustration which tends to embitter relations between rich and poor. The developing countries feel that their problems are ignored and they see no sign of real commitment to help to alleviate their tremendous problems of poverty, social change, and economic development. (ibid.: 78–9)

This report – by an Independent Commission established in 1968[5] – represents the conventional wisdom at the end of the 1960s. Dissatisfaction with the international institutions was thus already clear at this time.[6] The same criticism came a decade later in the Brandt Report, the next major statement of the 'international consensus' but by that time the international economic and political context had substantially changed (and the relative importance of multilateral financial assistance, notably from the World Bank, had increased substantially):[7]

> By the early 1970s the focus of debate had shifted away from aid to the structure of the world economic system. While the developing countries had benefited from the evolution of the international institutions, they wanted it to go much further. They maintained that the rules of the GATT were not sufficiently relevant to their special needs. They complained that the origins and initial power-structure of the Bretton Woods institutions limited the capacity for change, and they asked for a restructuring of the international financial system. (Brandt 1980: 39)

What actually occurred was very different. Throughout the 1970s, a new approach to development gradually took hold and was by the end of the 1970s firmly embedded in the policies of the major multilateral institutions. The structural adjustment programmes (SAPs) of the World Bank, described below, are the prime example of this way of thinking about development, where the emphasis was no longer on national planning and state-led industrialisation, but redirected towards market-friendly policies and macroeconomic fundamentals. The intellectual inspiration for the new approach to development was monetarist and neoclassical economics and the political philosophy of the minimalist state. This was the era of Thatcherism and Reaganomics, but several events in the early 1970s laid the foundation for the coming hegemony of neoliberal economics in multilateral institutions.

In order to understand the changing role and policies of the World Bank in this period, it is also important to take account of its relationship with the US Treasury, which became much more conflictual and problematic in the early 1970s. Robert McNamara was not the Nixon administration's preferred candidate for the presidency of the World Bank. He was seen as too unresponsive to the United States. When McNamara was appointed for a second term in 1972, the US support for him was lukewarm and came only after several European countries had made it clear that if America did not nominate McNamara they would advance a European alternative. It was also in this period that the United States cast its first vote against a proposed loan in the World Bank's Board. The loan was to Guyana and was opposed by the United States as part of a policy condemning expropriation of US private property (Gwin 1994). This vote was in accordance with what is known in US public law as the Gonzalez Amendment (Mingst 1990). As we will later see, the use of amendments to US public law to instruct US EDs to vote in specific ways in multilateral institutions has had a huge effect on the policies of these institutions.[8] The loan to Guyana was not the first World Bank loan that the US had been critical of, but this occasion represents the first time that the United States formally cast an opposing vote in the Board and thereby put its disagreement with the World Bank on public record.

The new more unilateral approach by the United States to the multilateral institutions was evident also in 1974 during the negotiations for the fourth replenishment of the IDA. The United States here became the first donor country of any considerable size to limit the increase in its contributions. Moreover, the United States demanded and got a number of concessions in order to take part at all in the replenishment round. Among its demands were: the establishment of an independent audit process for World Bank operations, due consideration of the US position in response to the expropriation of US private property in Peru (that is, the Gonzalez Amendment), and a substantial reduction in its share of IDA funding and an extension of its contribution over four years rather than the regular three. This last demand in particular was important, because it allowed the United States to hold its annual payment to the same level in current dollars as in IDA-3, while other countries made substantial increases in their contributions. The US approach to IDA-4 was a novelty in the multilateral system, but it was also the starting point of a continuing trend. Replenishment negotiations for soft-window facilities are now utilised by donor countries, either unilaterally or as a group, in order to promote specific issues or certain policies. In addition, the IDA-4 also represents the starting point for what has become the norm for US practice in multilateral institutions: minimum payment for maximum voting power. Such behaviour is not at all popular, but donors and recipients alike accept it because a multilateral institution without US participation would be a weak institution. Thus, with respect to voting power this approach has not had any effect; where it is noticeable is that other member countries, and also the multilateral institutions themselves, have taken over the role that the United States used to occupy: to conciliate, solicit and arrange compromises. This role is no longer occupied by one specific actor across the system of multilateral institutions, but varies from institution to institution and from issue-area to issue-area.

The dispute that emerged at the annual meeting of the World Bank in 1976 is not only a good example of the new unilateral activism in US foreign policy towards multilateral institutions, but it is also a good illustration of how early the US started to push what was to become the dominant development discourse of neoliberalism in the 1980s and 1990s. At this meeting, Secretary of the US Treasury William Simon countered McNamara's call for a general capital increase (GCI), with the assertion that the rate of World Bank borrowing and lending was growing too fast. Whereas McNamara argued for increased lending in light of the effects of the oil crisis and increased Third World debt, Simon drew attention to inflation and argued that the time had come for indebted countries to slow their borrowing and for developing countries to adjust their economic policies more to the logic of market forces. In Simon's statement at the 1976 annual meeting of the World Bank we find the same issues that were to dominate the development agenda of multilateral institutions in the 1980s and 1990s.

In considering how the present system might be improved to the mutual benefit of all nations, we should be guided by the following principles:

- Development by definition is a long-term process. Foreign aid can help, but such aid can only complement and supplement those policies developing countries adopt, which in the end will be decisive.
- The role of the private sector is critical. There is no substitute for a vigorous private sector mobilising the resources and energies of the people of the developing countries.

- A market-oriented system is not perfect, but it is better than any alternative system.
- A basic focus must be on increasing savings and making the institutional and policy improvements which will enable the financial markets to channel those savings into activities that enhance the opportunities for people to live better lives. (World Bank 1976: 190)

Here, in broad terms, we find much of the inspiration for the neoliberal agenda of the 1980s and 1990s and the structural adjustment programmes, but also for the broadening of multilateral institutions' policies towards governance issues. In particular the last of Simon's principles with its emphasis on institutional and policy improvements can, with hindsight, be read in this light.

In summary, by the end of the 1970s, major changes had occurred in the international economic and political order, and in the World Bank and other international institutions. After this time, it becomes far less meaningful to refer to these as a unified group. Rather, they must be treated as separate, and to some extent competing, entities – within a system in which the World Bank occupies a powerful position.

THE WORLD BANK: FROM STRUCTURAL ADJUSTMENT TO GOOD GOVERNANCE

The 1980s and 1990s in the World Bank may be characterised as a shift from structural adjustment to good governance. This process may be understood partly by reference to evolving experience (especially in Africa), but also by reference to the changing roles and rivalries of the major institutions: the World Bank, the IMF and the UN (primarily the UNDP). The shift may also be seen as a gradual broadening of the agenda: from the economic to the political.

When SAPs appeared for the first time in the 1980s, they seemed to represent a major departure from established World Bank philosophy and practice. But such changes do not take place in a vacuum; they are part of broader historical processes both within the institution in question, and in the external political and economic environment. The World Bank has never made unconditional loans. Even in the heyday of technical assistance when nearly all loans went to specific development projects (for example, road construction, building of dams), there were conditions to which the borrower had to agree, and some of these required adjustment and changes in national policies. The application of conditionalities was therefore not new. What was new was the broadening of the scope of the conditionalities attached to the loans. This broadening took place in a process which involved the three following components:

1. the change from project to programme lending. This kind of lending separates development finance from specific items of investment. A loan is given not for the purpose of conducting a certain development project, but as a general support for a balance-of-payments deficit to facilitate crucial imports (which will, it is hoped, increase economic growth in specific sectors and then spill over to the general process of national development);
2. the combination of programme lending with policy change conditions;
3. the broadening of these conditions from the sectoral or sub-sectoral to the national macroeconomic level.

It was the development in the 1980s of these kinds of mechanisms and techniques that represents the novelty, not the appliance of conditionalities as such. That said, these mechanisms increased the strength and scope of World Bank conditionalities. A simple definition of SAPs is therefore programme lending with policy-reform conditions that are economy-wide (Mosley et al. 1994: 28). The idea underlying the SAPs was that economic liberalisation is necessary for development, and the power that a multilateral institution like the World Bank has to grant and withhold aid money should be used to induce governments to liberalise their economies.

It is important to bear in mind that the World Bank was not implementing economic liberalisation for its own sake, but because it believed it to be the right development policy. The introduction of SAPs was not a conspiracy towards poor people in less developed countries, but an attempt to help. This attempt was both ideologically biased and lacked genuine knowledge and understanding about the specific features and internal logic of the states concerned (mainly in Africa), but it was still an attempt to promote development.

The economic turbulence in Africa and the second oil price shock of 1979 played important roles in the process that led up to the introduction of SAPs for borrowing countries, but it was more than a simple reaction to these events. It should also be noted that the internal World Bank process pre-dated the political landslide which returned conservative governments to power in the United Kingdom (May 1979), the United States (November 1979) and Germany (September 1980). These developments in the external environment clearly strengthened internal processes already under way, but originally the internal part of this process was mainly concerned with effectiveness and not ideology. There were several contributing factors.

Robert McNamara was reaching the end of his presidency and he wanted to be able to respond to critics such as Mahbub ul Haq who repeatedly argued that the alleged move to poverty-based lending was mere rhetoric, because the amount involved was too small to have more than a negligible impact on the well-being of the poor. McNamara's response came in the form of a proposal for a new programme of long-term programme lending.

On the operational side of the World Bank other concerns were more pressing. Here, the major issue was how to persuade borrowing governments to put their economic house in order. It was assumed that when this was done, poverty alleviation would automatically follow. Managers on the operational side had become increasingly disillusioned by the policy dialogue they were able to have with borrowing governments based on project funding, and were in search of new lending mechanisms upon which a stronger policy dialogue could be built. What were needed, therefore, were loans that were large enough to matter at the highest level of political authority – and policy conditionalites that were economy-wide in scope.

In 1980, a brief proposal document outlining the SAPs was presented to the World Bank Board and approved. However, even though the EDs in this respect bowed to the wishes of the World Bank's management, many of them were sceptical about the fruitfulness of the new approach, seeing it as a negation of the World Bank's previous claims about the effectiveness of policy dialogue through project lending. Many argued informally that if SAPs were what was needed, then the previous policy of project lending must generally have been a failure; but in the 1980s this discussion was never conducted openly. The scepticism of many EDs was widely shared among staff members. The introduction of SAPs was seen as a clear break with well-established lending principles not only in the World Bank, but in most other comparable multilateral institutions. The country-desk officers were perhaps those who most welcomed the new instrument because it could not only increase both their power *vis-à-vis* borrowing governments, but also enable them to bring rapid relief to customer countries that were distressed by external forces (deteriorating terms of trade, rapidly rising real interest rates, etc.). Although SAPs as a lending mechanism were established prior to the electoral success of conservative parties in Europe and the United States, it soon was regarded as an instrument to be used in order to pressure developing countries to follow orthodox liberal economic prescriptions of price reform and privatisation. Or in the words of the World Bank (1994a: 183), 'the state should not intervene where markets can work even moderately well'. This – the attempt by multilateral institutions to socialise and/or arm-twist borrowing countries into accepting a neoliberal mode for the organisation of their economies – is what later became known as the 'lock-in' argument (see Gill 1998; Taylor 2003).[9] We will later consider this argument in more detail, since it draws attention to an important aspect of the role that multilateral institutions play in the world political economy. There is however more to this picture than mere dominance and subordination. As Chapter 4 will reveal, the answer to the question of who is using whom for what purpose is never straightforward.

Structural adjustment

Between 1980 and 1986, approximately 37 SAPs were negotiated by the World Bank with various borrowing-country governments. These programme loans were given to countries prepared to undertake a programme of adjustment to meet an existing, or avoid an impending, balance of payments crisis. The SAP was supposed to be a 'response to a once-for-all, exceptional crisis in the balance-of-payments, albeit one that would require assistance over a longer period of time than that for which IMF stand-by finance was available' (Mosley et al. 1994: 40). In other words, the SAPs were supposed to solve the economic crisis that occurred in the majority of the African countries. They were devices designed to deal with Africa's unsustainable debt and general economic decline, which had resulted in hyper-inflation, chronic balance-of-payment deficits, currency crises and deterioration of public services. But they generally failed to achieve this purpose.

Initially, the World Bank argued that adjustment programmes had a favourable impact on economic performance and that 'strongly' adjusting countries performed better than countries with 'weak' or no adjustment programmes (World Bank and UNDP 1989). These statements were quickly challenged in a number of critical reports and reviews. Among the most influential of these, mainly because they used the same data-set as the World Bank, were reports by the United Nations Economic Commission for Africa (UNECA) and articles from scholars such as Paul Mosley and John Weeks. These reports and articles arrived at the opposite conclusion from that of the World Bank: countries with 'strong' adjustment programmes had a much worse economic performance than countries with a 'weak' or no adjustment programme. Such disagreement was not unexpected. But the evidence against structural adjustment was strong, and the case became stronger as the World Bank's praise for its own approach became increasingly muted – in the face of their own evaluations which identified many shortcomings and problems (Abrahamsen 2000). The first consequence of this was an attempt to make the pill of SAPs easier to swallow, by also including in the SAPs conditionalities aimed at creating social safety-nets for the poor. But the critics were still unconvinced both about the evidence and about the new social approach of the World Bank. At the end of the 1980s it was quite clear that SAPs had not been able to deliver what they had promised: a market-driven way out of poverty and misery.

There is a huge literature available about structural adjustment in Africa and elsewhere, and we see little point in revisiting this literature here,[10] but a few observations are appropriate as they have implications for our discussion about the change to the governance agenda.

One problem with many SAPs is what might be called the 'overload' problem. An average SAP included between 10 and 20 conditions about policy reform in specific areas, and some had as many as 100. The problem was that once a SAP was negotiated, it was very tempting for each different division of the World Bank to add additional conditionalities that reflected their internal priorities. This had many implications. One was the administrative overload it created for recipient countries. Most of these had weak state structures and bureaucracies, and it should have been obvious that there was really no way that the country in question could deal with the complex reform package that many of these programme loans constituted. The result was a kind of guessing game conducted by recipient governments: both those who never had any intention of fulfilling the reform conditions and by governments who originally had intended to do so but were unable to deal with all the reforms. What kind of conditions mattered the most for the World Bank? What kind of issue did one have to try to show some progress on in order to keep the loans one had achieved? The consequence was that instead of making it easier for the World Bank to monitor progress, it became much more difficult due to the multiplication of conditions and the guessing-game conducted by the borrowing governments. The whole process lost its initial clarity of purpose.

The frustration felt by the World Bank with SAPs is one important reason why the issue of governance so easily took hold in the Bank. At the end of this decade, in 1989, the Bank started to talk about a crisis of governance in Africa. There was a prevailing concern about the continuing lack of aid effectiveness, and a perception in the Bank that the African crisis was first and foremost caused by the low commitment to reform from borrowing governments and endemic corruption in developing countries (Santiso 2001a). The African patient was apparently unable, or unwilling, to take its medicine, and accordingly another approach was needed. The notion of governance offered both an explanation of why the economic growth it had predicted failed to emerge, and the elements of a new strategy.

Confronted with declining aid budgets and increased scrutiny by civil society organisations, the World Bank was forced to pay more attention to the pervasive effects of mismanagement and endemic corruption. However, there is also much more to the changes that took place in multilateral institutions in the 1980s and 1990s than just concern with aid effectiveness and mismanagement and corruption in borrowing countries.

'Governance' offered not only a new approach, but also an explanation of the World Bank's failure in Africa. The appeal of this concept for the Bank was that it implied that the African problem was not caused by wrong prescriptions made by the external donor, but by inherent weaknesses and failures in the governmental structures of African states. The state was the problem. This way of defining the problem was closely in accord with the by-then dominant economic paradigm of neoliberalism.

The introduction of governance into the World Bank's agenda also entailed a new interest in political factors among staff and management. This was a novel feature in the Bank, both because of the technical and functional approach that had been an integral part of the institution since its establishment, but also because the neoliberal orthodoxy of the 1980s completely ignored the political sphere and emphasised only economic issues. As such, the governance agenda represents a discovery of the political, and recognition that 'rolling back the state' is in itself not enough to stimulate economic growth. The governance agenda therefore clearly represents a widening of the scope of the Bank, but still within predetermined boundaries that at least in the foreseeable future will not be overstepped. The debate about governance is taking place within the framework of a technocratic consensus based on a functional approach to development. Likewise, it would be wrong to see the governance agenda as a break with neoliberalism. The ideal state is still a minimal state, but it is one which is highly efficient in carrying out economic reforms (Abrahamsen 2000). The governance agenda of the Bank is therefore best viewed as a continuation of the modernisation approaches of the past. Once more, the developing world, and in particularly Africa, is emerging out of this encounter as the backward other. Their task is still to become like us, but this time the means are not technical assistance for industrialisation, or structural adjustment of their economies, but the application of the Bank's good governance agenda.

This agenda was defined in narrow terms in order to fit within the already established framework of technocracy and functionality. Governance for the World Bank (1991, 1992, 1994b and 2000) therefore encompasses the form of political authority, the process by which authority is exercised in the management of a country's economic and social resources for development and the capacity of governments to design, formulate and implement policies and discharge functions. As such, the political dimension of governance is recognised by the Bank, but the operationalisation of the concept is restrictive. The question of how authority is exercised is seen as outside of the Bank's mandate. As a result, what is emphasised is the economic, management dimensions of governance. Good governance is defined as sound development management. Thus, the main part of governance-related activities carried out by the Bank has been public sector management, financial management, modernisation of public administration and privatisation of state-owned enterprises.

As we will see in the later sections, this has been the approach adopted by most multilateral institutions, precisely because they do not want to be seen as political, and have therefore always advocated a doctrine of neutrality. As such, they have embraced the functionalist logic that technical and economic questions can be separated from politics. The functionalist approach gives the illusion that technical solutions can solve political problems. In this way of thinking, 'politics is treated as a negative input into decision-making' (Grindle 2001: 370); it is seen as simply a manifestation of self-interest and rent-seeking behaviour which negatively distorts policy choices. Behind this idea is the view that people are in politics first and foremost for the promotion of self-interest rather than for furthering the greater common good. Governments should be viewed cynically and with caution, and often they have to be put under external pressure in order for them to implement certain policies (for example, economic liberalisation) that would improve the well-being of their populations.

The intellectual/ideological foundation for structural adjustment programmes, and governance, in the World Bank

Here we see how rational choice theory has influenced the World Bank's view of politics. Much of the analysis which constituted the foundation and framework for the SAPs in the Bank is based on this theory. The school of rational choice is linked to older theoretical contributions by scholars such as Anthony Downs (1957) and Mancur Olson (1965), but only made its way into the Bank in the late 1970s. In its earlier forms, rational choice theory was part and parcel of the positivist-functionalist social sciences that dominated the US academic world for the larger part of the post-Second World War period. However, it was first with the rise of neoliberalism that it found its way into the development discourse of multilateral institutions. In the World Bank it was in particular the works of Robert Bates and Douglass North that were cited. Rational choice theory provided the intellectual backbone for the neoliberal agenda aimed at creating an enabling environment for private investments.

The problem, in theoretical terms, with this way of thinking is that it is quite simplistic and one-dimensional. It fails to capture how politics plays out in a combination of struggles, not only over scarce resources but also ideas and values. For many World Bank staff, policy is essentially a sphere of rational analysis, whereas politics is dominated by irrationality (Santiso 2001). They therefore tended to assume that analysis and politics can be separated in the process of public policy making. This was the dominant mode of thinking in the Bank in the early 1980s. It was this approach which informed the Bank's approach to SAPs, and the consequences were huge. Today, this approach is still very much evident in the Bank's approach to governance, and the results from the recent emphasis on good governance programmes risk being as much in vain as the structural adjustment programmes of the 1980s.

We should, nevertheless, make it clear that the World Bank should not be seen as a monolithic neoliberal bloc, even during its most doctrinaire years in the 1980s and 1990s. The research department, which is seen by some as the intellectual heart of the institution, can at certain points in time be said to represent the extreme version of commitment to neoliberalism. To its critics, it seemed that the task of the department was not to break new ground empirically or theoretically, but to substantiate the case for economic liberalisation. Staff on the operational side, on the other hand, have been much more pragmatic in their views about developing countries and their prescriptions for them. In addition to the many research reports arguing for the neoliberal position, there are also many adopting a more pragmatic, or even contra-dictory view. And today, the World Bank is emphasising poverty alleviation and acknowledging its failure to mitigate the social costs of adjustment during the early 1980s; it has enshrined the lessons learned in its corporate philosophy. Nevertheless, the insti-tution as a whole – as opposed to specific individuals or sections within it – tends to adhere to and promote an approach which is at least economic-technocratic, and at most neoliberal.

The inclusion of good governance is not the only process of broadening of the agenda that took place in the World Bank in the 1980s and 1990s. Other issue-areas such as the environment, gender, indigenous peoples and involuntary resettlement were also taken up. We would suggest, however, that these were not the dominant themes – as perceived either by the Bank or the recipient countries – and may be seen as at best simply subsidiary issues, and at worst 'muddying of the waters' in policy terms. The case of the environment, however, is rather special; for, as we argued in Chapter 1 and will show in detail in Chapter 4, this issue became, through the activities of the NGO community and civil society at large, one of the major harbingers of change in multilateral institutions.

THE REGIONAL DEVELOPMENT BANKS

The adoption and implementation of new agendas by MDBs usually follow distinctive patterns. The traditional pattern is that the World Bank adopts new lending modalities and mandates on a global level at the initiative of donor governments and with the encouragement of NGOs (Nelson 2000). New mandates and institutions, such as governance and inspection panels, are often controversial and contested and evolve gradually as degrees of artificial consensus are created between donor member countries and important borrowing member countries. Similar processes are then repeated in the regional development banks. This is the usual pattern. However, there are several cases which do not conform; it would also be wrong to assume that if a process first took place in the World Bank it will automatically repeat itself in regional development banks. As we saw in Chapter 2, the regional development banks were established and exist autonomously of the World Bank. The membership of these institutions is different from that of the World Bank and so are their respective power structures and regional identity. In this section of the chapter we will explore the route that these institutions have travelled, from a narrow technical assistance agenda to a broader agenda including issues like good governance. Just as in the World Bank, a process of broadening has taken place, but within predefined parameters of technicality and functionality. Here also politics and economics remain unreconciled.

Regional development banks: the first decades (1960–80)

When the regional development banks (RDBs) started to operate in the early 1960s the main motive was to attract additional resource flows to their respective regions. The means to achieve this end was through technical aid. During the 1960s and 1970s these institutions were mainly involved in infrastructure, energy, agriculture and industry development. Even more than the World Bank they were engineering institutions. Development was about building something that was lacking, something that would take the regional borrowing countries one step closer to 'take-off'. Thus, in this period the RDBs gave primacy to resource inputs, and in particular, capital for investment, since capital was relatively scarce in their developing country member states. It was assumed that more investment would lead to higher economic growth (growth in GNP per capita), which for most of this period was widely accepted among multilateral institutions as the only development outcome that mattered (Culpeper 1997). What was important was the overall rate of growth of the economy. Who would benefit from growth, how growth would affect poverty and equality, were questions almost never asked in these institutions. Developing countries were seen as facing capital scarcity, while the industrial countries in the North were seen as capital abundant. Thus, the task of the RDBs was to overcome the capital market failure of their specific regions. They were to be agents that facilitated the transfer of private capital from an abundant North to a capital-starved South.[11] This understanding of the world and their place in it explains the centrality of investment, loans and the balance of payments in the discourse of these institutions in this period. More than anything else they were regional development *banks*, as the following example concerning Africa indicates:

> But most of all, the AfDB is a bank. It shows in its style of management, in its conservative approach to the risks of borrowing and lending and in the watchful eye it keeps on the performance of the loans it makes. Loans which the Bank extends to member states are, after all, a source of income for the Bank. While it is not the purpose of the Bank to make profits, the Bank's management never lose sight of the fact that the ADB must make its own way in the world, and to do that, the loans it makes have to perform. (*African Business*, January 1994: 19)

In the Asian Development Bank (ADB), the emphasis was on economic growth and cooperation rather than social progress. In the early years, the only exception was the Inter-American Development Bank (IDB). This bank began its life in the 1960s with a slightly different focus than the World Bank. The IDB provided loans to farmers and for social overhead projects (for example, water and sanitation, urban development and housing), as well as infrastructure, industry and mining (see Tussie 1995). The reason for this early venture into the social sectors is mainly the political motivations behind the creation of the IDB: the United States was eager to avoid repetitions of the Cuban Revolution elsewhere in Latin America. Nevertheless, despite some early indications of an interest in social development there was little coherent effort in the RDBs toward developing poverty reduction strategies until the 1980s. In the first 20 years of their existence, these banks were for all intents and purposes traditional development bank institutions with an emphasis on the kind of projects that their borrowing member countries found most interesting. These were projects concerned with industry, infrastructure, agriculture and irrigation, and energy. All these three institutions were in general favourably viewed by institutional investors who saw them as cautious and conservative lenders, but behind the scenes some of these institutions were becoming increasingly politicised. A prime example is the African Development Bank (AfDB).

When the AfDB was established in 1964, the majority of African member countries were opposed to soliciting membership from non-regional countries. However, in 1977, due to the meagre resources that a development bank comprised only of African member states was able to raise, the Board of Governors asked the Bank's management to start analysing this issue. At the next annual meeting, in 1978, it was decided to allow management to start negotiations with potential non-regional member countries. In 1979, amendments to the Bank's Charter were made. However, the ratification of these amendments required the consent of at least two-thirds of the member countries and of countries with at least 74 per cent of total voting power. It took three years to achieve this, as some countries, in particular Algeria and Nigeria, were reluctant to ratify the amendment. The reasons for this were ideological, but also geopolitical. In particular, Nigeria wanted to make certain that no new non-regional member country would be able to challenge the Nigerian leadership in the AfDB. A compromise was finally found in 1982, but rivalry and mischief (real or perceived) between Nigeria and leading non-regional countries has ever since been a recurring element in the AfDB. The political history of the ADB and the IDB are calmer than that of the AfDB, but even these institutions had their share of internal political controversies in this period. However, these internal controversies and politicisation apart, the first 20 years of the regional development banks were marked by a steady increase in their financial strength through fund replenishments and general capital increases. They received very little public attention and were more or less left in peace to facilitate their programmes of creating economic growth through infrastructure and industrial development. In the 1980s this was about to change, and here as elsewhere in the multilateral system it was increased public attention to environmental issues which became the harbinger of that change.

Environment and other cross-cutting issues in regional development banks

In an influential study published in 1979, Robert Stein and Brian Johnson made the observation that RDBs lacked any formal commitment to the environment or to specific procedures for considering environmental impacts in loans preparation and negotiation. But over the following years this situation began to change, and they experienced a series of challenges to their traditional development agenda. In the case of the AfDB, the first of a series of challenges emerged with the Francistown Abattoir Project in Botswana. In 1986, Botswana submitted a loan request to finance the construction and initiation phase of an abattoir to process and export meat products. In addition to a slaughterhouse and boning facility, the project also called for the construction of fences in order to enclose cattle prepared for slaughter.[12] During the planning process, environmental NGOs based in the United States started to raise objections to the project, based on a widely circulated film describing the disastrous effect on both indigenous and migrating species stemming from cattle fencing in Botswana that had been part-financed by the World Bank.[13] The area in question, Francistown, lies in a region with several national wildlife reserves, and the NGOs were worried that the AfDB would repeat the mistakes of the World Bank. The claim from the American NGOs and in particular from the National Resources Defence Council (NRDC), which headed the campaign, was that the project would lead to overgrazing and desertification (Shaw 1991). The NRDC brought its objections directly to the Bank, sending letters of concern to the President, but it also made use of its access to the US Treasury, and started a huge public campaign against the project in the United States. The aim was to get the Treasury to instruct the US ED in Abidjan to vote against the project. The campaign caught the attention of the media to the degree that even George Bush, Sr (then vice-president) decided to conduct a personal 'field study' of the project since he happened to be in Southern Africa anyway when the Francistown project hit the headlines in the United States. Bush Senior promptly demanded that his host, the Government of Botswana, took him, his advisers and the journalists that followed his Southern African tour, from Gaborone and up to Francistown.

The outcome of the campaign was a total fulfilment of the NRDC's objective: the US ED in Abidjan was instructed to vote against the project. This is but one example. Several projects and controversies emerged also in the ADB and the IDB. All of them contributed to making environmental policies a part of these institutions' permanent agendas. For a long time environment was seemingly the most important (and controversial) issue-area in the RDBs, but gradually other cross-cutting issues emerged which also challenged the traditional agenda of these institutions. This created controversies, but also confusion and ambiguity in institutions whose traditional way of life and view of their role in it were suddenly faced with demands for taking on tasks which could potentially turn everything upside down. The 26th Annual Meeting of the ADB held in Manila in May 1993 illustrates this. This meeting was marked by two main (and interlinked) events: (1) the ADB came under increased pressure to improve its project performance, and (2) the US opposed a general capital increase, which led to more tension than ever between the United States and Japan.

The background for the controversies that emerged was that even though internal studies showed that the project failure rate was increasing, the ADB was calling for donors to approximately double their authorised share capital to US$46 billion by 1998. The response from the donor community, and in particular from the

Clinton administration's top delegate, Jeffrey Shafer, was negative. Shafer argued that the ADB could not just raise its lending every year – the plan called for a 21 per cent rise in 1993 alone – without an objective appraisal of what everyone was getting for their money. He therefore called on the ADB to focus more on improving quality on loans rather than expanding the quantity. Such arguments against capital increase did not please Japan which strongly came to the ADB's support. According to the Japanese governor, Yoshiro Hayashi (Japan's Minister of Finance), both the Ministry of Finance and the Japanese government had 'high regard for the vigorous efforts that the Bank has made to restructure its organisation' (*Far Eastern Economic Review* 20 March 1993: 53). Nevertheless, even the ADB itself had to admit that the quality of its loans was declining. The figures released at the Annual Meeting showed that the number of 'successful' projects was falling. The ADB, however, argued that the reason for this decline was not poor management, but the fact that the ADB now had to conduct increasingly complex projects in countries where institutional constraints and lack of resilience to deal with external factors had adversely affected project performance. ADB officials even complained at the meeting that projects evaluated were picked randomly and included many 'soft', socially-oriented projects rather than solid traditional infrastructure projects which the customers (that is, borrowing countries' governments) favoured, and where success was much more easily achieved. Thus, according to the ADB, the problem with the quality of its loan portfolio was not general but highly specific. The problem for the ADB, however, was that the only countries that wanted change were the donor member countries. If the ADB could have it their way, they would be pleased to return to the 'golden days' of traditional projects, and just forget all the hassle with environment, gender, indigenous peoples, governance and the rest of the cross-cutting issues. In their view, these issues were forced on the ADB (and the other RDBs) by non-regional donor countries.

Malaysia was therefore applauded by most regional member countries (apart from Australia, Japan and New Zealand) when its delegates announced at the Annual Meeting that Malaysia had decided not to accept funding from the ADB for a highway project. Malaysia was to finance the road itself instead. The background for this event was a loan request from the Malaysian government to the ADB for financial assistance for the Sarawak part of a highway across Borneo. The problem emerged when it became known that the road construction work threatened the habitat of the Sumatran rhinoceros, an endangered species of which only a few were thought to be alive in Borneo. Under pressure from environmental NGOs who were aware of the ADB's new environmental policies, the Bank had to raise the issue of the rhino with Kuala Lumpur. Much to the delight of several developing member countries, the answer from the Malaysian government was 'Forget it; we will finance the project ourselves without all the hassle that your new guidelines and policies will cause for us.' Not only environmental issues, but also the demand for new policies on issue-areas such as indigenous peoples, involuntary resettlement and governance created divisions between donor and borrowing member countries in the RDBs. Due to the power structures in these institutions which give voting power majority to regional member countries, these kinds of conflict became very acutely felt. The continued problem for the management of these institutions was how to balance between donor countries (often under pressure from NGOs and civil society) which sought to implant new issue-areas in their agenda, and borrowing member countries which often openly resisted these same issues. Formally, the regional member countries were in the majority in the boards of these institutions, but it was the donor countries that controlled the resource flow. Without them there would be no capital increases or replenishments of the development funds.

A related problem was that these institutions were not very well equipped to deal with the new and increasingly complex agenda that was more or less forced upon them. After a while the RDBs learnt to handle environmental issues in a relatively adequate manner. But when further cross-cutting issues emerged, which entailed an integrated approach which could link them all together, the RDBs found themselves in trouble. It was no longer just a matter of finding the right technical approach to a functional problem. It was now a matter of finding solutions to increasingly politicised issue-areas. Instead of just financing a road, the RDBs were now supposed to ensure that the road also was of benefit to poor communities, and even to women in particular. Environmental issues were to be taken into consideration, but so too were issues concerning governance, indigenous people in the area and questions concerning resettlement. It is precisely these kinds of challenges that have brought the RDBs' managements into a difficult situation, squeezed between donors who call for what often seems like a never-ending line of reforms and new policies, and regional (borrowing) member countries which oppose the new direction in which donors seek to move them. This situation has been an important feature of the politics of these institutions in the 1990s and in the first part of the new millennium.

Governance is but one example. As will be demonstrated in Chapter 4, this issue-area emerged in the RDBs in the mid-1990s. As a concept, it was promoted by non-regional donors, resisted by most borrowing member countries and half-heartedly accepted by the institutions themselves. When the issue first surfaced, the message from the RDBs was that as *banks* they could only use the term (governance) in an economic context, and not in a political one. From their point of view two things were clear: whilst governance as an issue-area could not be avoided, governance as democratisation, individual political rights and human rights had to be avoided if the RDBs were to remain within the limits of their respective charters. In order to find ways out of all these conflicting views and opinions, the RDBs ended up approaching governance with an emphasis on collective economic rights and sound development management (that is, effectiveness and efficiency). This was the only approach to governance that donors and borrowers could agree upon.

In the next chapter we will return to the politics of these institutions, and in particular the political games that are played out around new issue-areas such as governance, environment, involuntary resettlement and the inspection function. Here it will suffice to say that the agenda of these institutions has been broadened, but that this has taken place within their traditional functionalist and technocratic approach to development. But, as the agenda became increasingly complex, the policy-making procedures of these institutions started to lose coherence, taking on the appearance of exogenous streams flowing through their internal systems, marked by arrival and departure times linked to specific opportunities and events confronting decision makers. This made the process of political manoeuvring between extra-regional and intra-regional demands and claims increasingly difficult.

THE WTO AND THE IMF:
SUSTAINABLE DEVELOPMENT AND GOOD GOVERNANCE

GATT/WTO and the IMF are, as already noted, not development institutions *per se*, but, especially during the last decade, we have witnessed increased congruence between these two and the multilateral institutions explicitly concerned with development. And this is not surprising. On the one hand, there is no doubting the importance of international finance and trade for poor countries, and hence for the World Bank, the RDBs and the UNDP. On the other, the WTO and the IMF have recognised the importance of the good governance agenda, and (following on events in the World Bank and the RDBs in the early 1980s), the WTO has been pressured to tackle sustainable development issues. We will briefly explore why and how this happened.

GATT/WTO and the environment

In GATT, the predecessor to the WTO, no explicit reference was made to the environment.[14] In 1972, GATT was, however, asked to report to the UN Conference on the Human Environment (UNCHE) which was held in Stockholm the same year. GATT's report *International Pollution Control and International Trade* constituted a strong reflection of the dominant free-trade paradigm in GATT (Nördström and Vaughan 1999).The basis of GATT's approach to trade and the environment was that trade had to be protected from environmental measures and not the other way around (Lund-Thomsen 1999). As a follow-up to this report, it was decided that GATT should establish a Working Group on Environmental Measures and International Trade (EMIT). This group was supposed to review all kinds of trade-related aspects of measures for pollution abatement and preservation of the human environment (Nördström and Vaughan 1999). This group, however, only existed on paper. GATT did not adopt the notion of the environment in its work or otherwise follow up on UNCHE, and EMIT did not meet until November 1991. In fact, in almost all other comparable multilateral institutions, the idea of sustainable development was firmly established by the time the idea was finally also taken up by GATT/WTO (Bøås and Vevatne 2003).

Already in the 1980s, the World Bank and other multilateral institutions were strongly challenged on sustainability issues by international environmental NGOs. GATT, however, did not receive much attention from these organisations. GATT was therefore able to continue the Uruguay Round without making any references to sustainable development in the negotiations.[15] The main reason for this, we suggest, was the low level of public awareness of both GATT and the environmental impact of world trade. There was a low level of public attention to GATT, and no formal relations between GATT and civil society organisations, and therefore hardly any pressure at all on GATT to address environmental issues. The traditional, technical and juridical approach to international trade (law) could therefore prevail. However, in the early 1990s GATT's traditional approach, or rather lack of it, came under fire from two sides. The European Free Trade Area (EFTA) countries, and in particular the Nordic countries, started a process at the Brussels Ministerial Meeting in December 1990 with the aim of bringing the work of the World Commission on Environment and Development (WCED) into GATT; and in the United States, the outcome of the tuna–dolphin dispute between the United States and Mexico raised public awareness of the trade–environment nexus in general, and in particular of the position and role of GATT within this nexus.

The root of the tuna–dolphin case is the US Marine Mammal Protection Act,[16] enacted in 1972. This law requires the US government to take steps to curtail the incidental killing of marine mammals by commercial fishermen, both domestic and foreign. Specifically, this law instructs the Secretary of Commerce to prohibit the importation of tuna products from countries whose dolphin 'kill ratio' (dolphin deaths per net dropped) exceeds that of US fishermen by a certain margin. In 1988, Earth Island Institute, a California-based NGO, sued to enforce this law, and a federal judge agreed that the US government was failing to uphold the law and ordered Mexican tuna imports to be banned from the United States. Mexico then asked for a GATT dispute settlement panel to adjudicate the matter. In September 1991, the panel concluded that the United States was in violation of its GATT obligations. This decision provoked heated debate over the fairness of trade and environmental conflicts.

Influenced by the WCED's report, the EFTA countries worked hard to include sustainable development on the agenda of GATT. Their proposal was not enthusiastically received, and in particular,

Brazil and India 'strenuously fought the GATT efforts to reinvigor-ate EMIT' (Esty 1994: 181). In the end, however, it was accepted that the environment was an issue for debate within the framework of GATT. The main reason for this was probably the *Zeitgeist*: the UN Conference on Environment and Development (UNCED) to be held in Rio in 1992 was already under preparation, and too outspoken opposition to sustainable development by GATT could therefore entail considerable political costs. GATT had also been asked by the UN to report to UNCED on the trade–environment nexus (see GATT 1992). This task was delegated to EMIT which then met for the first time ever in 1991. None the less, EMIT had very little influence on the Uruguay Round.[17]

The environmental NGOs were instrumental in the last stages of the Uruguay Round. The United States, particularly, was pressured by strong national environmental NGOs not to accept a free trade agreement which contained no reference to the envir-onment or the idea of sustainable development. The result was that the United States threatened not to sign the Uruguay Round Agreement if environment and sustainable development were not included. The United States made it clear that a reference to sus-tainable development had to be made in the treaty and that a committee on trade and environment had to be established. If not, the US argued that the strong domestic environmental opposition that the government was faced with would make it impossible to secure a majority in Congress for the ratification of the Uruguay Round Agreement. Thus, from the last negotiation meeting in December 1993 to April 1994, when the agreement was signed in Marrakech, the United States prepared the ground both for a separate statement on trade and the environment, and for a direct reference to sustainable development in the preamble of the agreement that established the WTO. The outcome was that in the final act of the Uruguay Round (April 1994), sustainable develop-ment was included in the rules of the international trade regime through the so-called 'Marrakech Ministerial Decision on Trade and Environment'. At the Marrakech Ministerial Meeting, the Dec-laration on the establishment of a World Trade Organisation was agreed upon and a reference to sustainable development was included in the preamble of the new organisation:

... allowing for the optimal use of the world's resources in accordance with the objective of sustainable development, seeking both to protect and preserve the environment and to enhance the means for doing so consistent with (the parties') respective needs and concerns at different levels of economic development. (WTO 1994)

The Marrakech meeting also established a much more formal Committee on Trade and Environment (CTE). The summaries of CTE meetings are posted on the WTO's website, but the committee itself is very much under the influence of the WTO's general culture of secrecy (see Bøås and Vevatne 2003). The meetings are conducted behind closed doors and NGOs are not allowed to participate in them. Even other multilateral institutions – such as the United Nations Conference on Trade and Development (UNCTAD), the United Nations Environment Programmes (UNEP) and the Organisation for Economic Cooperation and Development (OECD) – have only observer status and were allowed only to make formal contributions after the Singapore Ministerial in 1996 (Nördström and Vaughan 1999).

In the CTE, there has been a substantial difference between OECD countries and non-OECD countries with respect to the kinds of items and issue-areas on which they have submitted papers. One example of a North–South cleavage is that not one single OECD country has submitted papers on the export of domestically prohibited goods, while Nigeria on behalf of several other African countries has pushed this issue in GATT/WTO since the early 1980s.

The dispute settlement mechanism and the environment

The dispute settlement mechanism has become the new centre of attention for NGOs concerned with the environment.[18] However, this alternative route of access to the policy-making process of the WTO is also strewn with barriers. The failure of the WTO to clarify the procedural rules for submitting *amicus* briefs to the Appellate Body is an important indicator in this respect. The dispute resolution hearings are closed and very secretive. The decisions are taken by trade lawyers and economists, who do not have much knowledge about environmental problems, and the Appellate Body, that interprets and assesses the dispute panels' reports in accordance with International Law, has changed the outcomes of several disputes.

Despite these institutional barriers, some moderate environmental NGOs have had a certain degree of influence on the handling of environmental disputes (see Vevatne 2000a). One example is the shrimp–turtle dispute.[19] In this particular case, the WWF and the Center for International Environmental Law (CIEL) submitted *amicus* briefs to the dispute panels. These briefs were rejected, but they reappeared as an attachment to the statement paper of the United States. Here the NGOs did have quite substantial influence in the end, but this was much more due to their ability to lobby American policy makers in Washington DC than the openness and willingness of the WTO to hear their claims.[20] In this case, the Appellate Body supported the United States, and thereby also the environmental NGOs on a number of issues. In particular, the NGOs welcomed that the Appellate Body acknowledged that the sea turtle was a non-renewable natural resource close to extinction and thereby fulfilled the conditions of GATT article XX(g). And, even more important, the Appellate Body for the first time emphasised that WTO agreements had to be interpreted in light of the reference to sustainable development and environmental protection contained in the preamble to the WTO. The NGO community saw this as an important decision. However, their victory was only partial because even though the Appellate Body did find that the US law in question (Section 609 of the Environmental Species Act (ESA)) was a legitimate attempt to protect the turtle, the implementation and design of the law was not. Even more important in this case, however, is the fact that the briefs from the NGOs were rejected by the WTO. The only reason they reappeared was due to the ability of the WWF and CIEL to influence American decision makers.

Seattle and Doha

The large number of people who voiced their opinion about the WTO on the streets of Seattle not only delayed the start of the meeting, they also very successfully drew media attention to both the WTO in particular and international trade issues in general. The demonstrations had little direct impact on the negotiations, but they contributed to increasing the divergence of interests and opinions within the WTO, and thereby also helped cause the failure of the Ministerial Meeting and the launching of the Millennium Round (Fitzpatrick 1999; Vevatne 2000b).

The actions of the NGOs and the collapse of the negotiations underscored several significant weaknesses both with respect to the WTO's transparency policy and the procedures and practices of WTO negotiations. After Seattle, it became generally accepted that the WTO had to address these issues. As Remi Parmentier from Greenpeace International put it: 'The WTO has two options. Either its next meeting is in Pyong-yang, North Korea, to avoid the protests from civil society or it changes its attitude toward public scrutiny and democracy' (quoted in Fitzpatrick 1999). In fact, it was difficult to find someone willing to host the next Ministerial. In the end a candidate was found, but the choice of Doha, Qatar, as the host of the Ministerial in November 2001 seemed quite strange if the WTO really is committed to deal with these criticisms. To hold its Ministerial in the middle of the desert, in a country with limited rights to speak and demonstrate, illustrated the WTO's lack of understanding of the seriousness of the challenge from the Seattle event. The experience from the Doha Ministerial proves the point. The WTO described the next round of trade negotiations supposedly started in Doha as the *Development Round*, but according to more critical observers the outcome of the Doha meeting was nothing more than a 'shameless victory for spin' (*African Business*, January 2002: 10).[21] Already prior to the meeting, the negotiating text had been drawn in Geneva without much participation from developing countries. In Doha, immense pressure was exerted on poorer countries by the powerful trading nations who threatened to withdraw aid and debt relief, among other things, in order to get their way. The EU, in the teeth of opposition from the developing world, succeeded in pushing the environmental agenda. Most developing countries see this as little more than green protectionism for European and North American industries and a further attempt to keep exports from the poor world out of Northern markets. From the point of view of many a government in the developing world, the NGOs which have pushed the environmental agenda in multilateral institutions are a menace, and may even contribute to their seemingly permanently impoverished status. In their view their attempts at industrialisation are effectively disrupted by green protectionism implemented by Northern governments and encouraged by the

NGOs. (The questions concerning legitimacy and representation that such an argument raises are discussed in Chapter 4.)

The IMF and good governance

In July 1997, the IMF Executive Board approved new lending guidelines that instruct the IMF to withhold financial assistance to member countries with 'poor' governance. But the interpretation of governance they adopt is very narrow. As justification for this, they cite the 'political non-interference' provisions of the IMF Articles of Agreement. But this also implies that they will not withhold assistance to countries with poor human rights records. As critics would put it: IMF assistance can apparently be withheld on grounds of financial mismanagement, but not for state torture and murder.

One reason why the IMF has favoured the adoption of (an albeit narrow interpretation of) the governance agenda may be that it fits with the IMF's attempts to reconfigure economic territories in accordance with the above-mentioned macroeconomic paradigm and the opening-up of markets to foreign capital. Michel Camdessus, the then head of the IMF, was quite clear about this, asserting in 1998 that 'in a world in which private capital has become more mobile, there is mounting evidence that corruption undermines the confidence of the most serious investors and adversely affects private capital inflows' (quoted in Taylor 2003). Camdessus also made claims to a consensus over what such good governance was, saying that 'a broader consensus has emerged on the central importance of transparency and good governance in achieving economic success' (Camdessus 1998). Indeed, the IMF's own prescriptions for designing 'good governance' structures draw upon what it refers to as broadly agreed best international practice of economic management (see IMF 1997a). This 'best international practice' is, essentially, that of neoliberalism. But in order to really understand the IMF's adoption of the 'good governance' agenda we have to go back to the early 1970s.

It was at this time, with the demise of regulated exchange rates, that the IMF lost its main *raison d'être*. This provoked various attempts to find a new role, which have increasingly stimulated the institution to involve itself in affairs that many observers see as beyond the remit of the IMF's original mandate, that is, the IMF is indulging in 'mission creep'.[22] Facilitated by the debt crisis of the 1980s, the IMF began to emerge as an important player in the debate about governance and restructuring of national economies. The debt crisis was extremely important in this regard because the IMF emerged as the lender of last resort. At the same time, there was growing concern in many multilateral institutions that the structural adjustment programmes that had sought to reconfigure economies in Africa and elsewhere had been prevented from doing so by 'poor' governance. Instead of questioning their own prescriptions, most multilateral institutions instead sought to advance 'good' governance as a necessary precondition for reforms to finally work (see Taylor 2003): 'Governance provided a new toolkit, an instrument of control, an additional conditionality for the time when the traditional blame-the-victim, defence again becomes necessary. It further offered the opportunity to instil Western political values in borrowing countries and to fault them if things go wrong' (George and Sabelli 1994: 142).

In 1996, a declaration entitled 'Partnership for Sustainable Global Growth' was adopted by the IMF's Interim Committee, and in August 1997, a report promulgated by the IMF's Executive Board asserted that the IMF must henceforth assist member countries in creating systems that limit the scope for *ad hoc* decision making, for rent seeking, for undesirable preferential treatment of individuals and organisations. The ability of the IMF to promote its narrow, financial/economic interpretation of governance was made all the greater since, in the aftermath of the debt crisis, almost all other potential sources of credit – bilateral, multilateral or private – required an IMF stamp of approval before credit was given. State administrations were repeatedly 'advised' that economic recovery was dependent upon what was vaguely termed 'business confidence', and that this depended on a disciplined labour force and a state that pursued 'good governance'.

The IMF has therefore increasingly promoted what is often referred to as 'second-stage restructuring' (centred on the ideas of good governance) after it became apparent that many of the initial restructuring programmes were not working in accordance with plans.[23] The actual practical change from first to second-stage restructuring preceded the formal policy papers and statement on governance made by the IMF's board and top management. According to Kapur and Webb (2000:2): 'Through 1982, less than 5 per cent of IMF upper tranche arrangements contained 11 or more performance criteria' (that is, conditionalities related to governance). By the end of the decade, more than two-thirds of such arrangements had eleven or more criteria. These new additions to the IMF's concerns can be seen as a continuum of policies designed to remake states. Poor governance has been blamed as the central problem. Thus, the IMF's second-stage restructuring is targeting several dimensions simultaneously. IMF policies are designed to lock in state administrations to economic liberalisation, whilst at the same time giving the reforms a veneer of legitimacy based on liberal legal principles (Taylor 2003). As the IMF itself explains, 'the IMF has found that a much broader range of institutional reforms is needed if countries are to establish and maintain private sector confidence and thereby lay the basis for sustained growth' (IMF 1997b).

CONCLUSION: POLICY CHANGES IN AND AMONG MULTILATERAL INSTITUTIONS

There is little doubt that important changes have taken place in multilateral institutions. Not much more than a decade ago it was quite unthinkable that issues such as governance, sustainable development, indigenous peoples, social development and so on should occupy major positions on the agenda of the multilateral development banks, let alone the IMF and GATT/WTO. But we should also not overestimate the real extent of the broadening of the agenda, which is still going on. The failure of multilateral institutions to understand and take account of the political implications and dimensions of development, and thereby also of their own activities, is the major constraint here. We are of course aware of the non-political charters of these institutions, but they are, in practice, largely a facade. They prevent multilateral institutions from addressing human rights abuses, but allow them to address issues of corruption and management. They allow considerable and substantive interference in a county's choice of administrative structures and macroeconomic policy, but allegedly keep politics at bay. The problem is that whereas the agenda itself has been broadened to include many new issue-areas and tasks for these institutions, the institutions' understanding of development and definition of the relevant knowledge frame is still very narrow. It has not followed the broadening of their agenda. This means that multilateral institutions are ill-suited to deal with the new tasks that have been given to them. They are dealing with issues such as governance and sustainable development much in the same way as they dealt with building roads, dams and irrigation structures in the 1960s and 1970s: policies are seen as non-political and objective tools that, if correctly operationalised, will lead to improved project design that will in turn enable multilateral institutions to deliver on their promises of poverty alleviation and economic growth (combined with sustainable development and good governance). It is these misconceptions about the place of politics in development, and their role in developmental processes, that partly explain the increased criticisms against the multilateral institutions. More and more people have come to regard their reluctance to concede that their own role is political with disbelief and astonishment.

However, we also think that part of the reason for this inability to fundamentally reflect on their own role lies in the power structures in and around these institutions. These issues will be addressed in Chapter 4. Finally, we would like to draw attention to three major observations that can be drawn from this chapter. The first is how this process of widening the multilateral development agenda started in the World Bank and then quickly spread to the regional development banks, the IMF and the WTO. Second, the NGO community and civil society actors played an important role in this regard. This is an issue we will return to in Chapter 4. Here it will suffice to say that it is impossible to understand the politics of multilateral institutions without taking non-state actors into consideration. Closely related to this is our third observation, and this is the importance of the environment (and sustainable development) as the harbinger of change. The significant changes in policy making in multilateral institutions started when the NGOs entered the scene, and as we have seen and will again see in Chapter 4, it was the environment that was the issue that brought these non-state actors to centre-stage of the political process in multilateral institutions.

4
The Politics of Multilateral Institutions – Unpacking the Black Box

In this chapter we investigate the complex relationship between multilateral institutions, member states and (an increasingly important third party) NGOs. We do this largely by reference to specific case studies of processes which illustrate and to some extent have shaped the development of these relationships. None of these – the institutions, member states and NGOs – are homogeneous. We therefore exemplify and examine differences between multilateral institutions (for example, those with global as opposed to regional scope, and those with huge as opposed to modest funds for investment); differences between member states (donor or recipients, regional or non-regional members); and differences between NGOs (local or international, and advocacy or operational). We look at the interplay between these three types of actor, and to some extent also interactions within them (for example, between different departments).

We choose in this chapter to focus on case studies concerning the World Bank, the ADB and the UNDP, which represent the main types of multilateral institution. The case studies we have selected are largely concerned with the environment, which has not only been a central issue of debate in recent years but one which has contributed greatly to giving NGOs the power they now enjoy; and to a lesser extent with the issue of governance, which has also been controversial. Our main concern will be policy papers and project loan decisions (the two main manifestations of how policies are made, and put into practice). We will also refer to a relatively new and significant phenomenon – the Inspection Panel – and show how important changes have occurred in the Annual Meetings of the multilateral institutions, linked to the politics of protest, with which we end the chapter.

In June 1986, the United States cast its first vote out of concern for the environment against a World Bank loan. By late 1986 several other countries, including Germany, Sweden, The Nether-lands and Australia, were instructing their Executive Directors (EDs) to demand environmental reforms that echoed those urged by the United States; and only one year later, in May 1987, the President of the World Bank, Barber Conable, announced a series of organisational and operational reforms designed to respond to the new environmental concerns expressed by important donor countries. But where did this change come from? Was it just an example of powerful states taking a leadership in the multilateral system, or is there more to these processes than first meets the eye? In this chapter we shall seek to capture the political dynamics behind such processes of policy change in multilateral institutions. In doing so we will unpack the black box of multilateral institu-tions in a more thorough manner than we have done so far.

From the previous chapters it should by now be clear that it is a gross simplification to treat multilateral institutions as unilateral actors. What the board decides may officially be the policy of an institution such as the World Bank, but such policies are not developed by the board itself in isolation from the rest of the insti-tution. Rather, the policy paper or loan decision that the board reviews is the result of a long internal process that is influenced by a range of different historical experiences of the institution concerned. Secondly, policies once adopted are not fixed either in time or in context, but are constantly changing as they are put to the test and operationalised in relation to numerous projects and negotiations. They are multifaceted, and different departments and country offices within the institution concerned may modify and reinterpret them. This applies especially to the policy paper of a multilateral institution, whose purpose typically is to take stock of an issue-area. Their main function is to confirm and/or construct consensus; they are thus often discursive acts of consolidation rather than attempts to innovate.

The multilateral institutions themselves are, of course, major actors in these processes, but they are not alone. Involved in the politics of these institutions are member states, not only in the form of their ED but also through their home ministries; in addition, we increasingly find a third group of actors in the game, namely non-governmental organisations (related to, but not synonymous with, civil society). In this chapter we will analyse the interplay between these three groups of actors. How do they operate? What rules frame this relationship? How regular is their interaction? In order to do so we will refer to specific case studies. Some of these will also help us highlight both the potential and the challenges involved in civil society participation in the politics of multilateral institutions. Thus questions concerning legitimacy and representation will be asked, for in all relationships power is an issue, and we will therefore reflect on the often asymmetrical relationship between powerful international NGOs and local civil society organisations. In the final part of this chapter we will concern ourselves with what we define as the 'new' opposition to multilateral institutions and the 'politics of protest' manifested at annual meetings.

POLITICS IN MULTILATERAL INSTITUTIONS: A FRAMEWORK

The field of politics in multilateral institutions is a highly complex one. Member states are obviously important, but there are significant differences between the member states not only with respect to strength (for example, voting power and economic contribution to the system), but also concerning their ability and willingness to engage actively with the institution in question. Multilateral institutions have a considerable power to set the agenda, which normally takes place within their already established knowledge frame. Knowledge is power in multilateral institutions, and these institutions market themselves as the best reservoir of development expertise. But increasingly NGOs also are playing important roles within this field. They exercise their influence both through various branches of government and directly through multilateral institutions. The following case study, of an environmental project financed by the ADB, illustrates how the field of politics in multilateral institutions is socially constructed through continuous interaction among the three sets of actors: the multilateral institution, the members states and NGOs. The process examined below is not unique to the ADB, but common to most multilateral institutions. The IMF and the WTO (which do not finance projects) are clearly exceptions, but even these two institutions have been influenced by the debate that controversial projects like this have stimulated.

The ADB has for many years been involved in the energy sector, and as early as 1991 it seemingly demonstrated its commitment to sustainable development, when it informed the public that it focused its activities within this subsector on the development of indigenous and renewable energy resources. But in the case of the Masinloc Power Plant Project in the Philippines, the ADB confronted an alternative interpretation of its activities. This is a case of civil society opposition buckling under the weight of government pressure (Friends of the Earth Japan 1997), but it is also a story about a project that challenged and changed strategic thinking in the ADB headquarters.

The controversial issue was the location of the power plant. The 600-megawatt coal-fired thermal power plant was to be located at a pristine site. According to Friends of the Earth Japan (1997: 67), the community who lived there had developed a livelihood based on sustainable management of the area's mango trees and the bay's fish resources. For the NGOs, the local community was a model of successful community development, and this tropical 'paradise' was now threatened by an ADB-sponsored project. The ADB, they claimed, was definitely not promoting sustainable development, but ruining it. What made these events so important for forthcoming policy debates and institutional developments in the ADB was the negative publicity that the project generated. Opposition and protest by a coalition of local residents and national and international NGOs delayed the Masinloc project for almost four years. The NGO campaign even managed to get the Export-Import Bank of Japan (JEXIM) to promise that it would not co-finance the plant with the ADB unless the project was shown to be completely socially acceptable. Despite the continued resistance, the ADB and the Philippine authorities started the bidding round for the generator in October 1993. In order to defeat local opposition the Philippine government resorted to 'carrot-and-stick' approaches: making relocation offers to appease grassroots members while adopting police tactics to intimidate leaders.[1] In the end the local opposition succumbed and agreed to move. Supported by Japanese NGOs, some residents toured Japan and called on JEXIM to honour its initial promise, but this attempt also proved fruitless. On 22 December 1994, JEXIM announced its decision to co-finance, and in mid-1995, the final opposition vanished when the last of the local owners agreed to relinquish their property. Seen from a local point of view all efforts had been in vain. The power plant was built and the local residents lost in their combined struggle against the ADB, JEXIM and the Philippine government. As such, the campaign was also a defeat for the national and international NGOs which had been involved in the campaign against the project. But this campaign had wider ramifications, for the project also ended up representing a disgrace and a 'loss of face' for the ADB. In particular, the ADB found it extremely embarrassing that its co-financing partner in Japan, JEXIM, made a public statement against the ADB and the project. In the end, the ADB had managed to secure the outcome that it desired, but it turned out to be a Pyrrhic victory. It therefore became clear to some of the Bank's top-level management that it could not afford too many projects like Masinloc in the future. Some institutional changes had to be implemented in order to show to the world that the ADB's dedication to social responsibility and sustainable development was serious. For a long time these had been issues for debate in the ADB between non-regional donor countries and regional borrowing countries (with Japan trying to accommodate both sides), and also internally between project departments and policy departments. Non-regional donor countries and the policy depart-ments wanted to broaden the ADB's approach to include in a more coherent manner issues concerned with social responsibilty, local participation and sustainable development; whereas regional borrowing member countries and projects departments favoured a more narrow and traditional focus on providing technical assistance and funds for energy, industry and infrastructure projects. The Masinloc project shifted the balance between the parties. Japan wanted to avoid a repetition of the events of the Masinloc campaign and redefined its position on several of these issues, more in accordance with the approach of the non-regional donor countries. This gave increased weight to the arguments of the policy departments in the internal ADB debate. The institution has since then spent considerable time and resources trying to change the mix between its traditional activities and projects aimed at reducing poverty, developing human resources and protecting the environment. Since Masinloc, the ADB's goal has been to achieve a roughly 50/50 blend between the 'hard' and the 'soft' side of its development agenda. In the ADB's 1993 budget the first tentative steps were taken towards the implementation of this policy, but this has been an extremely difficult and controversial process because leading regional member countries (all of them major and reliable borrowers like China, India and Malaysia) were not at all pleased with these developments. They have repeatedly stated their opposition and resistance to them. In the ADB, as in most other multilateral institutions, this debate is therefore still unresolved.

In this case we are again confronted with three different sets of actors – member states, institutions and NGOs – but none can be displayed as unitary actors. Member states must be divided between donor member countries and borrowing member countries; but, since this is a regional development bank, we must also distinguish between regional and non-regional countries. In general (for example, in the AfDB and the IDB), regional member countries are not donor countries. But this is not the case for the ADB. Here we have one very powerful regional donor member country, namely Japan (and in addition also Australia and New Zealand). In some multilateral institutions, a member state also occupies a near-hegemonic position. The United States is always a country constituency in itself, and the role of Japan in the ADB should not be underestimated. Some member countries, are part of country constituencies but dominate their groups totally (for instance Nigeria in the AfDB), whereas other countries even though they continuously control the ED position, interact with other country constituency members on an equal basis (for instance Canada in the ADB). In addition, some countries' contributions may overall be quite small, but they may be very important within certain sectors and issue-areas. An example of the latter is the role played by the Nordic countries in support of environment and gender issues. The main point is that the balance of power between the three groups of actors varies considerably across multilateral institutions. And this variance is important if we are to understand what is going on within these institutions. We cannot treat them equally, either for advocacy or for analytical purposes; we must understand their differences as well as their similarities.

Another important factor regarding the structures of power in multilateral institutions is their geographical location. The role and might of Japan is significantly greater in the ADB than in the

World Bank (although it might have been even more had the ADB been based in Tokyo). But this is further complicated by the question of whether the institution is regional or global. Both the IDB and the World Bank are located in Washington DC, each within a 15-minute walk of the US Treasury. Yet most observers would argue that the US has exerted less power over the IDB than over the World Bank (see Jerlström 1990; Bull 2002; Bull and Bøås 2003). Why is this so? One explanation is that, at least formally, regional development banks are controlled by regional member countries. Different institutions have different power structures, and differences in power structures also influence internal debates between various offices and departments in different ways. The governance debate in the IDB is markedly different from that in the World Bank, even though both institutions are located in Washington DC.

NGOs, also, are far from uniform. We have to separate between local, national and international NGOs, and also differentiate between operational NGOs and advocacy organisations. The former are engaged in project work, often together with multilateral institutions, and therefore tend to be both better regarded by multilateral institutions and borrowing governments and also more receptive to their views. By contrast, advocacy NGOs tend to be much more critical of the policies and approaches of multilateral institutions. The tables below set out, in summary form, the most important distinctions. This is a useful framework to bear in mind as we examine the politics of multilateral institutions by reference to further case studies (see Table 4.1).

Table 4.1   Multilateral institutions

	Scope	Decision-making structure	Types of country constituency
World Bank	Global	Weighted votes	1 country, dominant country, rotating chair*
ADB, AfDB, IDB	Regional	Weighted votes	1 country, dominant country, rotating chair*
IMF	Global	Weighted votes	1 country, dominant country, rotating chair*
UNDP	Global	1 country, 1 vote	no country constituencies
WTO	Global	1 country, 1 vote	no country constituencies

* that is, the Executive Director comes from a different country in each new period.

Table 4.2   Member states**

	Borrowing country	Donor country
Regional member	Many (e.g Nigeria)	Few (e.g. Japan)
Non-regional member	None	Several (e.g. Germany)

** Table 4.2 relates only to regional development banks. In the case of the World Bank and the UNDP, a few countries are formally both donors and lenders. In practice this means, that they still are repaying old loans, for example Japan, which remained on the World Bank's list of debtor countries until 1990 (see Orr 1990).

Table 4.3   Types of NGOs

	Local§	National§	International
Advocacy	Very many	Very many	Many (e.g. Greenpeace)
Operational	Very many	Very many	Many (e.g. Care)

§ The number of NGOs at local and national levels is very high in total, but varies enormously from one country to another.

States, foreign policy and multilateral institutions[2]

In its foreign policy with regard to multilateral institutions, a member state may be seen to play one of four possible roles: lead state, supporting state, swing state or veto/blocking state (see Porter and Brown 1996).[3] A lead state has strong commitments to a certain issue-area, makes serious attempts to move negotiation processes forward, and actively seeks support from other member states for its preferred solution. A supporting state speaks and acts in favour of proposals from a lead state, whereas a swing state is one that demands substantial concessions to its point of view as the price for agreeing. A veto/blocking state is one that either openly opposes an agreement or tries to weaken the agreement to the point where it is more or less useless for its original purpose. The stronger a member state is (in economic, political, military terms), the more able it may be to fulfil any of these roles. The potential for exercising effective leadership varies somewhat according to various items on the agenda of multilateral institutions, but the United States is clearly the one actor which no multilateral institution can afford to ignore in the long run. When the United States is actively engaged in trying to forge international consensus, it can often overwhelm other states that have taken on the role of swing states or veto/blocking states. Alternatively, when the US role is that of the swing state or the veto/blocking state, the agreement in question is inevitably weaker. The interesting question that arises from the next case study is whether the NGO community can significantly influence the role of the United States (to act as a lead state instead of a swing state, or veto/blocking state) in its foreign policy on multilateral institutions.

NGOs are often given credit for putting environmental issues on the agenda of multilateral institutions. World Bank meetings have been a focal point for NGO activity at least since 1983, when six large US NGOs pressured the World Bank to include environmental costs in its projects (Aufderheide and Rich 1988). This event was followed by criticism of World Bank involvement in 'scandal' projects such as the deforestation caused by the Polonoroeste project in Brazil, the soil erosion and resettlement problems related to the Narmada Dam project in India and the deforestation and social consequences of the Indonesian transmigration project (Wade 2003). The controversies around these projects entailed much public criticism directed against the World Bank, and even threats of reduced financial contributions emerged (Bøås 2001b). NGOs based in the United States focused on, and criticised, the World Bank's involvement in these projects. They lobbied both the World Bank and the US Congress, and in June 1986 the first 'no' vote based on environmental considerations was cast by an American ED for a World Bank project (Harboe 1989).

Not all NGOs are able to play – or are interested in playing – a role in the processes that we will document here, but those who do so can be compared to transnational corporations. They have a home base, they have foreign affiliates, and they often enter into strategic alliances both with other international NGOs and with local and national NGOs when they operate abroad. WWF, Friends of the Earth (FoE), Environmental Defence (EF), International Rivers Network (IRN), National Resources Defence Council (NRDC), BothEnds and the Sierra Club are all examples of international NGOs with the power of making their cases heard both domestically (for example, in the US Congress) and internationally (for example, in multilateral institutions).

The Pelosi Amendment

The secretary of the US Treasury serves as the US governor on the boards of governors in the various multilateral institutions, and the US EDs in the World Bank and the regional development banks are usually also recruited from the Treasury. With respect to multilateral institutions, the prime target for US NGOs, on the administrative side of the US government, has therefore been the Treasury. The Treasury's assistant secretary for international affairs also chairs the Working Group on Multilateral Assistance which was established in 1978 to coordinate US policy on multilateral institutions, and which meets weekly to discuss positions on upcoming loan proposals and policies. All loans and new policy proposals are assessed on the basis of whether they are in accordance with general foreign policy, as well as whether the projects are seen as properly conceived by American standards. The decisions reached in these meetings are transmitted to the EDs and must be followed closely.

Equally important from the NGO point of view is the monthly informal meeting between the international environmental NGOs and representatives from the Treasury, the State Department, USAID and the Environmental Protection Agency (who review upcoming environmentally controversial loans). Although these meetings are informal in style, they are in fact formalised in US public law through legislation passed by Congress in 1986 to establish an early warning system.[4] Two NGOs, the Sierra Club and the NRDC, conducted the drafting of the legislation that inscribed the Early Warning System into US law. The objective of this system is to provide advanced notification about projects thought to pose environmental problems, and to publish a list of these projects every six months (Bøås 2001b).

On the legislative side of the US government, Congress has been an important channel of influence for the NGOs. At the request of the National Wildlife Federation (NWF), the Environmental Policy Institute (EPI), and the NRDC, six different congressional subcommittees held extensive hearings on multilateral institutions in 1983–84. As a consequence of these hearings, the Treasury conducted a study of the environmental policies and practices of multilateral institutions and, in particular those of the ADB, the IDB and the World Bank. This study was submitted to the House Banking Subcommittee on International Development Institutions and Finance. On the basis of this study, the subcommittee held a new round of hearings in close consultation with US-based international environmental NGOs in order to review a series of draft recommendations concerning multilateral institutions and the environment. The outcome of this new round of hearings was that the subcommittee urged the Treasury to strengthen its monitoring of environmental policies in multilateral institutions and, just as important from the NGO point of view, to expedite the flow of information between multilateral institutions, Congress, other relevant federal agencies and the public. The US EDs in multilateral institutions were called upon to press their respective institutions to work with NGOs. They were also urged to vote against any projects that would result in unacceptable environmental damage, which was defined by the subcommittee as unsustainable resource exploitation, species extinction, pesticide misuse, degradation of protected areas and disturbance of the habitat of indigenous peoples (Rich 1985). In December 1985, Congress enacted these recommendations into US law.[5]

Following these events, the Sierra Club started to spearhead a campaign with the objective of making it impossible for US EDs to support funding of any proposed project from a multilateral institution that could have a major impact on the environment unless an Environmental Impact Assessment (EIA) was made available at least 120 days in advance of board consideration. The Sierra Club focused its lobbying on the House Banking Subcommittee on International Development Institutions and Finance, as well as on strategic members of Congress. Among those targeted, the most important legislators to win over were Representative David Obey (who was chair of the Appropriations Subcommittee of Foreign Relations, which controls House bills for funding multilateral institutions) and Senator Robert Kasten (who held the similar position in the Senate).

The original idea for the EIA law did not stem from Congress or Senate, but from the international arm of the Sierra Club. Larry Williams, the leader of this section of the Sierra Club, took the idea to one of his close associates in Congress, Representative Nancy Pelosi. Williams' suggestion was that she and the Sierra Club should draft a bill that would require multilateral institutions to adopt an EIA process in exchange for the US vote. Such a bill was written by Larry Williams and the Sierra Club, signed by Nancy Pelosi, and handed over to Congress.

The US Treasury, which until then had been supportive of the environmental concerns of the NGOs, strongly opposed legislation proposing an EIA 120 days in advance of any project. The argument of the Treasury was that multilateral institutions would not be responsive to such a law; the United States would be prevented from supporting a majority of future requests and thereby lose much of its power to influence policy and loan decisions. The counter-argument from the Sierra Club was that no multilateral institution could afford to have the United States excluded from participation in loan decisions; they would therefore move quickly to implement the EIA requirements rather than risk the loss of US funding. The US NGOs seemed more confident of American power than was the US government itself.

The Treasury objections did not stop the Sierra Club's campaign. In legislation passed in 1988, the secretary of the Treasury was directed to promote environmental reform of multilateral institutions by requiring US EDs to take recommended positions and report back to Congress on compliance, and USAID was required to monitor projects likely to have an adverse environmental impact.[6] In 1989, the Sierra Club finally won when Congress passed legislation directing the secretary of the Treasury to instruct their EDs not to vote in favour of any proposed action by multilateral institutions that would have a significant effect on the environment, unless an EIA was completed by the borrowing country or the lending institution. The multilateral institution had to make the EIA available to Board members at least 120 days in advance of Board consideration, and either the full EIA or a comprehensive summary available to affected local groups and local NGOs also at least 120 days in advance of Board consideration.[7]

With hindsight, it is obvious that the Sierra Club's assessment of the situation was the correct one. The Pelosi Amendment did not exclude the United States from policy making in multilateral institutions; quite the reverse. Indeed, this is an excellent example of the hegemonic power of the US in multilateral institutions. Within one year, a US law was turned into standard operating procedures not only in the World Bank, but also in the regional development banks. The Pelosi Amendment therefore demonstrates how domestic law can be turned into international 'law' (practice) not under governmental direction, as state-centric literature on US hegemony suggests,[8] but by a non-governmental organisation. In this case, the policy of the United States was directed not by the US administration, but by an external non-governmental agent – the

Sierra Club. This suggests that any genuine understanding of the hegemonic power of the US or other actors has to penetrate beyond state capability in a narrow sense and consider the relationship between state power and domestic agents with the ability to influence international agendas and outcomes. It was NGO activism that changed the role of the United States from a swing state to a lead state in this case. The NGOs provided leadership, not the US administration. There is no doubt that US commitment to the environmental agenda strengthened the position both of other member countries who advocated environmental reform of multilateral institutions, and the agents of such reform within these institutions.

The Pelosi Amendment and the subsequent translation of US law into international standard operating procedure constitute important milestones in the history of multilateral institutions. But the enactment of this legislation did not constitute the end of NGO pressure on multilateral institutions and influence over state power. Access to formal authorities and decision makers is an asset, but it can also have the character of a double-edged sword. Later in this chapter we will return to this issue and discuss questions concerning legitimacy and representation in light of the framework for critical engagement that we established in Chapter 1. The most important question at this stage, however, is what this case can tell us about the politics of multilateral institutions.

There are two important lessons to be learned. First, some of the most important policy decisions do not arise from processes within the institutions themselves. The debate on environmental policies and environmental reform had been going on in these institutions since the early 1980s. Some progress had been made, but not much. In many institutions, and among many member countries, the commitment to this new agenda was, to put it mildly, lukewarm. It was only when this debate was transplanted from multilateral institutions into the deep heart of policy making in the most important member country that a political process was put in motion that ended up having system-wide consequences for the activities of multilateral institutions. This act of transplantation was not undertaken by an agent of the government of this country, but by a non-governmental actor. The final outcome, however, was then transplanted back into multilateral institutions through the new directives sent out by the US government to its various EDs.

Second, this illustration exposes the necessity of conducting a 'multiple unpacking' if we are to understand policy making in, and the politics of, multilateral institutions. Not only can we not treat multilateral institutions as unitary actors, but the same is true with regard to member countries. In order to untangle the politics at play we must also expose the internal political processes in the member countries that are most relevant to the case that we are investigating. Often the United States is one of the countries concerned, but this is certainly not always the case.

In summary, in order to analyse the processes under study, we have to understand the internal workings not only of multilateral institutions but also of member states. Some NGOs have become very skilled at doing so, and it is time that analysts and other concerned parties learnt from their lead. The following examples from the ADB and the World Bank provide apt illustrations both of the internal politics of multilateral institutions and the broadening of their agenda that has taken place – albeit within well-defined borders.

GOVERNANCE AND CROSS-CUTTING ISSUES: THE FINE ART OF POLICY MAKING IN MULTILATERAL INSTITUTIONS

Arun III was a proposed hydroelectric scheme in Nepal. A 201-megawatt hydroelectric project was to be built on the Arun River in a remote part of the Nepalese Himalayas at a cost of approximately US$1 billion, or about twice Nepal's annual national budget. Involved in the preparation of this project were the ADB, the World Bank, and the bilateral aid agencies of Germany, Japan and Sweden.[9] For the approximately 40,000 people from about ten different ethnic groups who inhabited the Arun Valley the project would entail new economic opportunities, but the dam and the proposed 118-km road that were to be built would also entail major cultural, economic and environmental change. The project itself, however, would only involve the displacement of some 155 families, because the design would not require the construction of a large water reservoir. For the donors, bilateral and multilateral alike, this seemed like an uncontroversial project.

Nonetheless, soon after the plans were known to the public, there emerged a coalition of national and international NGOs opposed to the project. They formed a campaign network called the Arun Concerned Group. This network was formally coordinated by a Nepalese NGO called INHURD International, but it is now generally recognised that the real facilitating actors were the Environmental Defence Fund (EDF)[10] and the International Rivers Network (IRN). The NGOs argued that the proposed project was both too expensive for Nepal and also both socially and environmentally unacceptable. The hydro-power project, they argued, would destroy the world's last genuine Himalayan forest valley: the pristine forest could be seriously harmed, and this would entail extinction of the area's already endangered plant and animal species. Among these were the Asian black bear, clouded leopard, Asiatic golden cat, jungle cat and scaly ant-eater. All these represented images of exotic and endangered nature easily communicated to a Western public. The NGO coalition also argued that the project road to be constructed would open the area to illegal logging operations, that the migration into the Arun Valley of an estimated 40,000 workers and their families would lead to social disintegration, and that the local and indigenous people in the Arun Valley had deliberately been misinformed about the project.[11] This last point of NGO criticism was directed toward the bilateral partners to the project, such as Germany and Japan, whom it was claimed were only in it for the money. In sum, the argument was that bilateral donors with the support of the World Bank and the ADB had railroaded the Nepalese government.

The strategy of the NGO coalition was conducted along two parallel tracks: lobbying in Nepal and in the United States. The aim was to delay the project so much that it would no longer be economically sound. There were two reasons for this: first, the World Bank had already let it be known to the public that even just one year's delay would add US$25 million to the cost of the project (*Financial Times* 22 October 1994), and secondly, the NGOs were aware of internal World Bank opposition toward the project. One section of the World Bank endorsed a more cautious approach, and argued that the World Bank should perhaps rethink the whole design. It was argued that the project might be simply too large for Nepal, and that it would not develop Nepalese capacity; the World Bank should therefore look for alternative ways of increasing energy production in Nepal. The Washington DC-based NGOs were well informed about the internal World Bank debate, and tried to use it for their own purposes. One central part of their strategy was therefore aimed at increasing the internal division in the World Bank over this issue (Friends of the Earth Japan 1997). In order to achieve this the NGOs filed a motion to the World Bank's Inspection Panel. Here, they requested that the project be abandoned on the grounds that it violated the World Bank's own policies and procedures.

The World Bank Inspection Panel is a new phenomenon, important for a full understanding of the political processes with which we are concerned. It was established in the aftermath of the controversies surrounding the World Bank's involvement in the Narmada Dam Multipurpose Hydro project in India, in order to deal with complaints from external parties. After several years of NGO activism and engagement with the World Bank and its member states, the World Bank suspended its support for the Narmada project in 1993 (see Wade 2003). The Arun claim was the first to be filed to the World Bank's Inspection Panel, and member states, NGOs and the World Bank all eagerly awaited the outcome of the case.

In August 1995, the World Bank, much to the astonishment and anger of the Nepalese government, announced that it would withdraw from the project. Whether or not they had been railroaded into the project by donors, they certainly were railroaded out of it. However, for the World Bank and its president James Wolfensohn, the concerns and anger of the Nepalese government were of less concern than the international image of the World Bank in important donor member countries (in particular, the United States).[12] What was important for James Wolfensohn's decision was the recommendation from the Inspection Panel for the project to be inspected. This suggested that the World Bank might possibly have violated its own policies and procedures. This was not a situation the president could live with; he therefore basically had just one option left: to pull the World Bank out of the project.

After the World Bank pull-out, the other bilateral and multilateral donors also left the project. The Arun III Hydro-power project in Nepal was officially dead, but its termination had ramifications far beyond the borders of Nepal, and we here summarise some of the most important ones. What is particularly interesting is that they all point to an almost interactive process of policy formation between the NGOs and the multilateral institutions. Although member states are also, of course, actors in these processes, they are usually drawn in by lobbying and other forms of activity undertaken by non-governmental actors.

As noted, the Inspection Panel's function was established as a consequence of previous interaction between NGOs and the World Bank with respect to the Narmada project in India; but Arun III was the first test case of this function. This test proved that the NGOs now had at their discretion an institutional mechanism within the World Bank which they could use to challenge the World Bank on its own terms. For the World Bank, the Inspection Panel's function was important as an institutional mechanism for damage control and public relations. If at the end of the day an organisation finds itself fighting a losing battle it looks better to be able to say that we (for example, the World Bank) are an accountable and transparent institution, and if there is any chance we have made a mistake we will investigate it and if necessary rectify it (that is, initiate the Inspection Panel function and adhere to its findings). It is therefore no surprise that the ADB, the World Bank's multilateral partner in the Arun III project, started to develop its own inspection panel function as a consequence of the events described above. In the case of ADB involvement in controversial cases such as Arun III, the management concluded that public relations would be much better served if one could divert possible complaints to a formal institutional procedure (an inspection function) rather than trying to deal with such matters on an *ad hoc* basis. A further consideration, in the case of the ADB, was the role of the non-regional donor countries. The leadership of the ADB was concerned that an inspection function might be forced upon them, and it was therefore preferable to start this process on its own terms. One important outcome of Arun III was thus that the establishment of inspection panel functions spread from the World Bank to the ADB, and a debate on the need for such a function, in one form or another, spread to most multilateral institutions.

There are variations in how such a function is fulfilled, but the different institutions generally share much in common.[13] The official objective of inspection functions is to establish formal procedures for community organisations or other groups affected by *public sector* projects to assess whether the formulation or the implementation of the project were consistent with the policies of the multilateral institution in question.[14] The inspection function can therefore be applied to public sector loans, guarantees and technical assistance (TA) grants financed in whole or in part from either multilateral institution resources or resources administered by a multilateral institution. These may include projects under preparation, as well as projects that have been approved and are still under implementation. The group making a request for inspection has to present evidence that its rights or interests have been, or are likely to be, directly, materially and adversely affected as a result of a multilateral institution's failure to follow its operational policies and procedures in connection with the project concerned. Inspection requests can therefore only be made either by groups residing in the developing member country where the project is or will be implemented, or by a group in another member country adjacent to that country, if the group is likely to be affected by the project.

The group making the request will first have to take up its grievances with management. If the group is not satisfied with the response, it can then submit a request for inspection to a special committee located at the board of directors. This committee will then decide whether to recommend an inspection to the board of directors. The board will consider such a recommendation, and if the board then chooses to authorise an inspection, a panel composed of individuals from a standing roster of independent experts will be formed in order to carry out the inspection. The task of such an inspection panel is usually to identify all relevant facts, ascertain whether the multilateral institution in question has been in compliance with its operational policies and procedures, and recommend, if appropriate, any remedial changes in the scope or implementation of the inspected project. After receiving this report, the board will make the final decision on what kind of actions, if any, should be undertaken by the multilateral institution in question.

One important outcome of the events described here was therefore the proliferation of inspection functions across the system of multilateral institutions. As shown by the Arun III case, the existence of such a function can have a significant effect on the outcome – as NGOs and multilateral institutions lock horns with each other. Although they do represent an important step toward the overall goal of making multilateral institutions more accountable to the people affected by the projects and policies, a number of problems have been associated with them. It is apparent that the procedures are formalistic and bureaucratic. As presently constituted, many local groups, even if they are aware of the existence of such functions,[15] will not be able to satisfy the demands for evidence that most multilateral institutions have established. The burden of evidence is on the local groups. It is they who have to convince boards both that they are affected and that the institution in question has violated its own policies. This will be an extremely difficult task for most local community groups in developing countries (indeed, perhaps also in any country). This is why the few times that this avenue of protest has been attempted are when coalitions of international and local NGOs have been established. The Arun III case is an important example of the effectiveness of this kind of coalition building.

Another major problem with current inspection functions is that they are time-consuming. This means that in some cases the project in question can be finalised before any decision about either the establishment of an inspection panel or about the report from such a panel is taken. The case of the Samut Prakarn Wastewater Management project in Thailand illustrates this point. This ADB project, which we describe later in this chapter, is very controversial in many respects: environment, local participation and governance (that is, corruption) being the most apparent. The local community group that opposes the project has filed a request for an inspection panel, but this process has proven to be so time-consuming that it is quite likely that the project will be finalised before any decision on establishing an inspection panel can be reached. If this is the case, and later investigations reveal that the ADB in fact has violated its own policies, the legitimacy of inspection functions can be seriously questioned. This implies the need for serious reform, such that it becomes much easier to file requests for inspection panels by local groups, and, equally important, that projects in respects of which such requests have been filed should be temporarily stopped. Such procedures are, of course, both expensive and time-consuming for multilateral institutions; but it is difficult otherwise to justify the many words spoken about participation, accountability and transparency.

The debate about inspection functions which this project triggered off did not take place in isolation from other political processes within and between multilateral institutions. It must therefore be seen in relation to the wider debate on questions concerning governance, indigenous peoples and involuntary resettlement. It is to these issues that we now will turn, but before doing so, the reader should also note that Arun III may turn out to be the 'last great dam' of multilateral institutions. Following the Narmada experience, the World Bank had become sceptical about large dams, so that prior to Arun III many people in the World Bank were already of the view that there was just too much controversy and bad publicity around such projects. This was exacerbated by Arun III, leading to an even more widespread feeling that it was not worth getting involved in dam projects; it was impossible to avoid being caught in a public relations game in which the Bank was more or less doomed to lose.[16] The emergence of such an attitude in the World Bank and other multilateral institutions has huge ramifications, not necessarily positive, even seen from the point of view of environmental NGOs. One may argue that the abandoning of large dam projects by multilateral institutions is good for the environment both locally and globally; but it may also be noted that such a change in policy does not necessarily imply that such projects are not carried out. At least for middle-income countries it may simply mean that they are financed by private sources, without World Bank (or other) interference at all. This is perhaps good for the World Bank and other multilateral institutions because it spares them from bad publicity, but from an environmental and human development point of view the gains are more uncertain. When the Bank was involved, at least some criteria for environmental soundness and protection of locally affected groups had to be considered; when only private actors and national governments are involved, the standards adopted may well be below those of the Bank. This raises issues concerning legitimacy and representation to which we will return in a later section of this chapter. Before doing so, however, we turn to another major issue – governance – which has been somewhat controversial and which again illustrates the complex political dynamics between the three groups of actors with which we are concerned. We begin with the ADB, which is especially interesting because of the ambivalent position of key member states in this debate, before turning to the UNDP which has in recent years made a strategic decision to focus on this issue. Here, it is policy papers (on governance) rather than loan decisions (on major dam projects) which are the manifestations of policy.

Governance: whose agenda?

On 3 October 1995, the ADB became the first multilateral institution to establish a Board-approved policy on governance; but as we have seen from Chapter 3, this process started much earlier in the World Bank where it emerged in relation to what the Bank defined as the African crisis. Our purpose here is not to revisit this debate, but rather to try to examine what happened as the governance agenda spread across the system of multilateral institutions. The official adoption of the governance agenda is an important moment in the history of multilateral institutions, because for the first time these institutions adopted policy positions on issues that could be seen as challenging one of the key elements in the international system: namely the idea of national sovereignty. Recipient member countries feared that the new governance initiatives that materialised across multilateral institutions would infringe their national sovereignty and further politicise decisions regarding their loans. As a concept, governance was promoted by donor countries and resisted by borrowing countries. The following illustration from the ADB underscores this dilemma.

It was the Asian Development Bank's 1994 Annual Meeting that implanted the governance agenda in the Bank. The concept was promoted by non-regional donor member countries, resisted by most developing member countries (especially China and India), and half-heartedly accepted by the ADB itself and Japan. When the question about governance was first raised, the ADB argued that as a bank, it could only use the term 'governance' in an economic context, not in a political one. From the ADB's point of view it was clear that whilst governance as an issue-area for the institution seemed unavoidable, governance defined in terms of democratisation, individual political rights and human rights had to be avoided, if the institution was to remain within its charter of political neutrality. In order to try to find a way out of this maze of conflicting views and opinions, it was decided to commission a study of East Asian development experiences that would examine three specific aspects of governance, all of which were more concerned with collective economic rights than with individual political rights. These were:

1. the bureaucratic capacity to implement policies, programmes and projects;
2. the relationship between government and business – how to establish effective policy outcomes, and
3. the principle of shared growth, from which whole populations could benefit.

In April 1995, a Workshop on Governance and Development brought together development practitioners and scholars from six of the high-performing economies of the Asia region: Hong Kong, Indonesia, Japan, South Korea, Singapore and Taiwan. Not surprisingly, the dialogue at the workshop revealed considerable apprehension among the participants that an ADB governance policy would solely reflect donor preferences and experiences. They argued that existing definitions of governance, such as the one advocated by the OECD, reflected the experience and interests of Western donors (individual political rights) without taking into account important components of the Asian experience (collective economic rights) (see Root 1996).[16] In order to avoid this kind of Western bias in the ADB approach to governance, it was argued that knowledge distilled from the workshop should constitute an important part of the framework for an ADB policy paper on governance.

The question was therefore how to define governance in such a way that what was perceived as the concept's Western bias was avoided. The solution was found in the intricacies of the English language, and more specifically in the definition found in one of its most respected dictionaries, *Webster's New Universal Unabridged Dictionary*. This allowed governance to be defined as the manner in which power is exercised in the management of a country's economic and social resources for development. What made this definition so attractive for the ADB and its Asian member countries was that it linked governance directly to public and private management of the developmental process, and to collective economic rights rather than individual political rights. Thus, according to the ADB, governance encompasses the functioning and capability of the public sector, as well as the rules and institutions that create the framework for the conduct of both public and private business including accountability for economic and financial performance, and regulatory frameworks relating to companies, corporations and partnerships. In broad terms, then, governance is about the institutional environment in which citizens interact among themselves and with government agencies/officials. (ADB 1995: 1–2)

Under this interpretation, governance focuses almost exclusively on effective management. The emphasis is not on choosing 'correct' policies, but rather on their effective implementation.

If we compare this definition of governance with the one chosen by the World Bank, as we see below, the difference is not very significant. But there was a significant difference in the process leading up to this conclusion. In the ADB, this was much more politicised. The deliberate aim of the seminar that preceded the governance policy paper was to convince Asian policy makers that the ADB could find an Asian approach to governance, without the perceived Western bias that was evident, for instance, in the OECD perspective. This kind of open articulation of regional political space and resistance was not at all apparent in the World Bank; indeed it was something that the Bank would have to resist. If it were to modify its approach to take account of specifically Asian perceptions of governance, it would have to do the same for others too. In the mid-1990s, the Bank's approach to governance and governance-related issues was therefore cautious, as we have seen in Chapter 3. Such is the nature of policy making in the multilateral system; processes that may seem similar when viewed from a distance may embody unique characteristics when we look at them more closely. The governance agenda has become a universal agenda, but it is also an agenda on which different multilateral institutions seek to find their own niche.

The issue of governance relates very closely to the controversial topic of national sovereignty, so that different multilateral institutions have differing opportunities and constraints in terms of how and to what extent they can deal with it. In the eyes of many developing countries, the UNDP enjoys greater legitimacy as representing a diverse range of national views, at least by comparison with the World Bank; while the ADB occupies a complex, inter-mediate position: it is a regional institution, but one which is strongly influenced by views from outside the region. And finding one's own niche is not only about division of labour and cooper-ation between various institutions, it is also very much about institutional rivalry. The UNDP and the governance agenda offer an illuminating illustration of this point.

The UNDP and governance

As a major multilateral institution, the UNDP has played a central role in defining the field of development aid. And as is the case with respect to the other multilateral institutions analysed in this book, there is also a dynamic interplay between the UNDP and other actors in the multilateral system. The UNDP must be seen as part of a broader structure consisting of donor countries, recipient countries, other multilateral institutions, NGOs and also the media that all influence, and are influenced by, the policies of the UNDP. As we already have seen in Chapter 3, in the 1980s and 1990s the World Bank and the IMF deepened and broadened their role with their comprehensive policy prescriptions to developing countries. As a consequence, the World Bank in particular became increas-ingly active in what had been the UNDP's traditional field of action. Thus, in the 1990s, we witnessed a substantial change in the nexus between the World Bank and the UNDP. The space between them became a field for both cooperation and discord. The UNDP has far fewer resources than the World Bank, and when the Bank started to 'invade' UNDP territory, many UNDP strate-gists began to worry as to what would remain in their particular domain. At the end of the 1990s, the UNDP was therefore a mul-tilateral institution in search of a new purpose. They found the answer in governance.

On 1 July 1999, Mark Malloch Brown was appointed as the new administrator of the UNDP, and he immediately initiated a com-prehensive reform programme. The new vision to guide the UNDP into the new millennium was presented in Malloch Brown's *Business Plan 2000–2003* (UNDP 2000a). The UNDP was to transform itself from a development fund administration to a mul-tilateral development institution with the ability to stand at the forefront of the development debate. The promotion of good governance was the central tenet in this transformation, because this agenda was seen as the avant-garde of the debate. The primary activity for the UNDP was therefore to become the main policy adviser on good governance among multilateral institutions:

> As globalization brings the world closer together, it increases the need for programme countries to have a stronger capacity, good governance, and effective policies and institutions. The assets of UNDP position it to play a unique role in this venture. It is engaged in critical arenas of the global development agenda and at the same time has intimate knowledge of the practical problems that people and authorities in programme countries face on a day-to-day basis. As part of the United Nations, and thanks to its multicultural and multidisciplinary nature, UNDP has an impartial perspective that is unmatched by any other development organization. (UNDP 2000a: 3)

Thus, in his first year as administrator of the UNDP, Mark Malloch Brown constantly advocated a greater role for the organisation in policy dialogue and the good governance agenda. This was the path to institutional survival for the UNDP: 'In the uncertain situation facing multilateralism, and therefore, UNDP, survival depends on the ability to find innovative solutions to the serious problems of dwindling resources, increasing competition, and more sophisticated client demands' (UNDP 2000b: 11). As an agency in the multilateral system, the UNDP therefore had a clear interest in embracing the governance agenda, and this interest was mainly created by increased inter-institutional rivalry with the World Bank. The UNDP could not match the Bank in resources, but perhaps it could do so in the intellectual realm.

The relationship to the World Bank is something the UNDP has been concerned with for some time. Already in the period from 1989 to 1992, the UNDP kept the activities of other multilateral institutions under constant scrutiny, paying particular attention to the impact of new ideas and innovations within the field of development aid. As we have seen in Chapter 3, the World Bank started, in the early 1990s, to take into consideration issues of national governance in their policy dialogue with various member countries. This apparently significant reorientation generated two competing views in the UNDP. Some saw it as a 'refreshing departure from the past practice of ignoring the broader issue of national governance' (Haq 1995: 148). However, the World Bank's attempt to recreate its role in the multilateral system was also inter-preted as a strategic way of getting into the 'softer' side of multilateral development assistance, a field that the UNDP felt was its own. The increased fascination with good governance as a par-adigmatic solution to all developmental problems had profound effects on one multilateral institution's position *vis-à-vis* other institutions in the system. It appeared that the natural division of labour between the UNDP and the World Bank, which had char-acterised their inter-organisational relationship for decades, was vanishing as the World Bank (and even the IMF) began to play a broader and still more visible role in development.

This posed a challenge to the UNDP, to which it responded in two ways. On one hand, it sought to carve out its own profile in the multilateral system, but on the other it also tried to maximise its benefits from cooperation with the MDBs, and the World Bank in particular. As one observer put it: 'The World Bank is UNDP's major rival and partner'[18] and, in view of this, the institutional interaction between the UNDP and the World Bank can be seen as a process in which both institutions try to gain effective agenda-setting power. The governance agenda represented a new opportunity for the UNDP. A close look at the annual reports from the UNDP's administrator illustrates the central importance attached by the institution to good governance. In 1994, 1995 and 1996, significant sections of the annual reports were dedicated to governance issues. The quote below is a typical UNDP statement in this period:

> Looking back to the annual report for 1990, a comparison with the UNDP of that year and the UNDP of the present is instruc-tive. During the five-year period, the understanding of development itself has undergone a change in paradigm. The United Nations, in part through its series of global conferences, has been a major actor in this evolution. Specifically, UNDP, as the principal development arm of the United Nations, has made a significant contribution to this process through its emphasis on the people-centred nature of development and the importance of sustainability – both ecologically and institu-tionally. UNDP is recognised for its conceptual work on capacity development and the linkage with effective governance. (UNDP 1995: 13)

From 1995 and onwards, the UNDP has repeatedly referred to good governance as its central priority (Dam 2002). The good governance agenda was increasingly seen as the UNDP's competitive edge against the World Bank. With the appointment of Mark Malloch Brown as the new UNDP administrator in July 1999, this strategy was made explicit. A good example of this is the 2002 *Human Development Report* in which the main theme is good governance. This report examines a set of aspects that the World Bank does not include in its governance framework; a new and broader definition is proposed, including a 'human governance index', which explores economic, political and civic governance indicators. This is, according to the UNDP, in contrast to the more narrow conceptualisations utilised by the MDBs (UNDP 2000b).

Our suggestion is therefore that the UNDP's turn to governance as its main issue-area, and the subsequent broadening and reconceptualisation of the term, is mainly the result of the increased competition from the World Bank in the UNDP's traditional field. This exemplifies the point that a significant aspect of policy making in multilateral institutions is inter-institutional rivalry. The politics of multilateral institutions is a complex field. Many actors are involved in a quest for control and influence over different agendas, and the actors within these institutions are constantly under pressure from diverse interest groups. Politics in multilateral institutions is about exercising influence over highly complex agendas. And here, as in other political arenas, decisions taken at one point can lead to unforeseen consequences. The Samut Prakarn case from Thailand, to which we now turn, illustrates this clearly, while also demonstrating the increasingly complex agenda that multilateral institutions are facing as target populations start to take seriously the policy papers they publish on issues such as the environment, participation, involuntary resettlement and governance. This case study from 2002 illustrates a number of important aspects of the current situation: what are the significant divisions and power balances, how NGOs relate to multilateral institutions both directly and through the national level, etc. It also illustrates how an Annual Meeting can be strongly influenced by a specific, controversial loan decision which has wider implications for policy.

THE INSPECTION PANEL FUNCTION AND
THE ADB IN SAMUT PRAKARN[19]

At his opening address to the Board of Governors at the ADB's 35th Annual Meeting in Shanghai, China, 10–12 May 2002, Tadao Chino, the Bank's president, listed five key events of the previous year. One of these was the ADB's first inspection case, which had been brought to conclusion in 2001. According to Chino, the inspection process yielded many useful lessons for the ADB, and he told the Board of Governors that he had already created a steering committee and working group to review the ADB's Inspection Panel function; concurrent with this review, the Bank was also conducting a comprehensive review of its Operational Manual to ensure that it incorporated all relevant operations policies. In this process, Chino told the Board, the ADB was seeking the views of all stakeholders, including government officials as well as representatives from NGOs, the private sector and civil society (see Chino 2002). To many of the representatives from private banks and financial institutions this speech came as a great surprise. They wondered why Chino wasted time in this important opening address to the Board on what seemed to be an insignificant project in Thailand. The reason was that Chino had realised that the ADB was about to enter into a major public relations disaster in Asia concerning the Samut Prakarn project. This part of his speech was therefore all about damage control; by referring explicitly to the case he tried to regain the initiative on this particular issue. If the seminar the next day organised by the NGO Forum on the ADB was an indicator of his success, he failed to do so. The NGOs and local Thai representatives from the project area had little difficulty convincing prominent representatives from Asian and international media that this case had by no means been brought to a satisfactory conclusion. But what is this Samut Prakarn case all about? In order to understand this, and the implications it may have not only for the ADB but also for other multilateral institutions, we must return to 1996 when the ADB established its policy on an inspection function.

The ADB's Inspection Panel function was established as a consequence of its involvement with the World Bank in the Arun III project in Nepal. However, some would argue that it was not really meant to be used by the ADB in practice; its main function was as a showpiece for the donors. According to this view, the ADB thought that the process of filing a request for an inspection panel was so complicated and technical that the likelihood of a local group of people affected by an ADB project doing so in a successful manner was very slim; the decision makers had invented it for public relations purposes, not for it ever to be used against the ADB in practice. Five years later, this was, however, precisely what happened. It is worth setting out the nature of the project in some detail.

The Samut Prakarn Wastewater Management Project in Thailand is funded by the ADB and the Japan Bank for International Co-operation (JBIC). The intention of the project is to improve environmental quality and public health in the Samut Prakarn Province. The project is supposed to establish:

- wastewater collection and effluent monitoring systems,
- a central wastewater treatment plant,
- industrial pollution prevention and clean technology transfer programmes, and
- institutional capacity building for government agencies responsible for wastewater management.

There was no lack of good intentions behind this project, and few would dispute that Samut Prakarn is badly in need of improved wastewater treatment. For the ADB, the Samut Prakarn project, set to be the biggest facility of its kind in Southeast Asia, was intended to be a showpiece: a model of how the ADB was supporting environmental clean-up in a part of Asia that is heavily polluted. But events turned against them; and the managers in the ADB responsible for this region probably wish they had never heard of this part of Thailand. Allegations of corruption, abuse of bidding processes and violations of laws and policies have been levelled against the ADB, the Thai government and the JBIC. In particular, the residents of Klong Dan have been very active in organising a campaign against the ADB. The reason is simple: somewhere in the planning process, the central wastewater treatment facility was relocated from its original project site on Bang Pla Kod and Bang Poo Mai (on both sides of the Chao Phraya River) to Klong Dan, 20 km away. The people of Klong Dan were not informed about this, and no new environmental assessment was carried out (NGO Forum on ADB 2002).[20] At the 33rd Annual Meeting of the ADB in

Chiang May in Thailand, over 200 residents of Klong Dan converged, together with over 3,000 other demonstrators, at the conference site to voice their objections. During the Annual Meeting, the local representatives from Klong Dan met and made alliances with international NGOs such as the NGO Forum on ADB, the Bank Information Center, and Environmental Defence. These NGOs soon realised the multifaceted nature of the Samut Prakarn case and saw this as an opportunity to test the ADB's commitment to its own stated policies. From May 2000 and onwards, Samut Prakarn was no longer just a case of local resistance against the ADB, it had become an international issue. However, it is important to note that, unlike many other cases of alliance between local and international NGOs, in this instance the local representatives from the communities in Klong Dan were not taken over by the international NGOs for their own purposes. As far as we can judge, the local leaders are very much in charge of their own destiny.[21]

A much more coherent campaign was started in the aftermath of the meeting at Chiang Mai. The local activists and the NGOs wrote letters, issued policy statements, and staged protests at local, national, regional and international levels.[22] Their statements and protests revolved around four main issues, all of them potentially painful for the ADB: environmental concerns, efficiency, effectiveness and governance/corruption.

Concerning the environment, it was claimed that the project site is essentially a large bed of soft mud that is too soft to support such a huge construction. The filling of an existing drainage canal, necessary for the purposes of the project, may create pools of stagnant water, posing serious health risks. And the residents of Klong Dan, who depend on the marine resources for their livelihoods, feared that the plant would damage the coastal ecosystem on which their community and way of life depended.

The efficiency argument took as its point of departure the fact that the project cost had increased from 13.6 billion Thai baht at the original site to 23.7 billion Thai baht at Klong Dan. This price increase is due to the greater distance between the source of the wastewater and the treatment location, which resulted in more pipes being needed to channel the water to Klong Dan.

Objections were also raised over the effectiveness of the project in safely and adequately treating the wastewater, since after both pre-treatment and treatment, the water would still contain 5 per cent of heavy metals and hazardous chemicals. This contaminated water would then be released into the coastal areas of Klong Dan, threatening both local fisheries and people's health.[23]

The important and still unexplained change in project location led to allegations about corruption with regard to the purchase of land and the construction of the pipeline. According to the local activists and the NGOs, the Klong Dan site was purchased for an unusually high price, and more land was paid for than actually required for the project; they have suggested that the project was moved merely in order to create business opportunities for specific firms and individuals. Even more damaging for the ADB were the accusations made by the NGOs of close ties between ADB staff members and members of the Ministry of Science, Technology and Environment (MSTE) which, it was claimed, had pushed the project forward despite the social and environmental problems it would create.

The inspection complaint[24]

In addition to staging protests, the local activists, with the help of their international counterparts, also made use of the ADB's Inspection Panel function. On 29 November 2000, an official letter of complaint was sent from the villagers of Klong Dan to President Chino. After a long and controversial internal process in the ADB, on 10 July 2001 inspection of the project was authorised. A three-person Inspection Panel was established accordingly, charged with determining whether or not the ADB had complied with its operational policies. If the Panel found that the ADB had not complied with its policies, it would determine whether such non-compliance had, or was likely to have, a direct and material adverse impact on the rights and interests of the group making the request for the Inspection Panel.

The Panel began its work on 27 August 2001. It soon suspended its work – on 8 November 2001 – because it was not able to conduct a field visit to the project site due to the conditions imposed by the Thai government, which included a requirement that the ADB accepted liability for any loss damages claimed by the contractor resulting from the Panel's visit. In December 2001, the Panel submitted a final report to the ADB's Board Inspection Committee, which was a desk study – and therefore somewhat limited in scope. But it still concluded that the ADB had failed to comply with several of its policies, a critique which was very damaging for the ADB.

The Panel found that the ADB had failed to carry out a reappraisal of the entire project when the supplementary loan was made – when project costs increased due to the change in location of the project. The ADB's Operational Manual is quite clear on this issue: 'The procedures for processing a supplementary loan, whether by additional financing or by reallocating of funds from other Bank-financed projects, is similar to that for new loans, and includes reappraisal of the entire project.' The Panel believed that the failure to carry out a full reappraisal was the crucial factor from which most of the other problems followed. In addition to this, which was their major concern, the Panel also found the ADB to have violated seven other of its policies, including those on involuntary resettlement, the incorporation of social and environmental dimensions in Bank operations, and good governance.

In essence, what this meant for the local villagers was that the Panel found that their rights and interests with regard to consultation and participation had not been adequately respected. The Panel suggested that in order to establish an environment of trust with the people of Klong Dan the ADB should acknowledge noncompliance with some of its policies, and begin negotiations as soon as possible with the Klong Dan community on:

- the degree and extent of actual and potential damages and appropriate and adequate compensation for those affected,
- the remedial action programmes for immediate and longer-term solutions, and
- the participation of the local community in the management and operation of the treatment plant so as to minimise any future potential adverse effects on the community.

The Panel believed, however, that, given the current stage of the project implementation, suspension should not be recommended. However, the Panel also stated that if their remedial recommendations, including mitigation of the adverse effects of the project in a manner satisfactory to the local community in Klong Dan, could not be implemented, then disbursement should be considered suspended (as requested by the group that made the claim).

The ADB management's response to the conclusions of the Panel only added fuel to the fire. Many observers questioned whether the Inspection Panel function was meant for any practical purpose other than pacifying donor member countries. The Bank's management completely rejected the Panel's findings, defiantly maintaining that they had not done anything wrong, and that the Panel's recommendations were totally misplaced. Such an approach was doomed to backfire. As one senior donor member country official told the *Financial Times* (10 May 2002): 'The Bank reacted appallingly to the first ever inspection process. They went into corporate litigation mode, rather than the mode of a public institution being accountable. The total rejection of a report of an Independent Panel was to me unacceptable.' This was surely the main reason why President Chino mentioned the Inspection Panel function in his opening address to the 2002 Annual Meeting; he was trying to show that the ADB took its policies seriously.

After a lengthy discussion in the ADB between management and the Board's Inspection Committee it was finally agreed that the Bank should acknowledge that it had failed to comply with several of its policies and should start active discussions with the Klong Dan community. Much to the ADB's surprise, the Klong Dan community was not very interested in discussing the matter unless it led to a total suspension of the wastewater project. They wanted to continue to live the life they were used to, a point which the ADB apparently found difficult to understand.

The Samut Prakarn project was supposed to become a showpiece of what the ADB could achieve. Instead, the community's public airing of their anger and resentment turned Samut Prakarn into a public relations fiasco, exemplifying some of the main problems in the ADB's approach to its work, and particularly its close relationship with borrowing governments. The controversy around Samut Prakarn has also exposed deep divisions among the ADB's management, borrowing member countries and non-regional donor countries about the appropriate role of NGOs and civil society in monitoring bank projects.[24] Countries such as China and India argue that critics from civil society may simply undermine developing countries' progress by demoralising ADB staff. This debate is likely to continue, not only in the ADB, but also in other multilateral institutions with comparable power structures, as donors under pressure from civil society seek to make them change their ways. But changing a multilateral institution such as the ADB will be a slow, painful and contentious process, with borrowing-country governments likely to resist any change that they interpret as a potential infringement on their sovereignty. This debate (to which we will return in Chapter 5) will surely be a hallmark of multilateral institutions in the years to come, but there are also other important implications that we should consider from this case.

One of them concerns alliance-building between locally affected groups and international NGOs. The Samut Prakarn campaign is both the largest and the best organised ever against the ADB. Partly this is a consequence of the increasing size and organisational capacity of Asian civil society and its NGOs. However, it is still interesting to examine why Samut Prakarn became the first project to present such a great challenge to the ADB. In order to explain this we have to consider again the basic purpose of Annual Meetings. The Annual Meeting is more than anything else a meeting place. Originally these meetings were an arena for government officials, bankers and private and institutional investors busily 'networking', that is, moving, with an expensive glass of red wine in their hand, from one reception to another. Those were the old days. This element of the Annual Meeting still exists, but from the mid-1990s a new dimension has been added to these meetings. They have also become the rallying point for groups and people opposed to their policies. And these groups and individuals network as well. This was precisely what brought Samut Prakarn to the world's attention. Prior to the Annual Meeting in 2000, which was held in Chiang Mai in Thailand, few people outside of Thailand were aware of this project at all. When the Thai government proposed to host the meeting in Chiang Mai, the idea was of course not to provide a rallying point for the local activists from Klong Dan, but to bring government officials, bankers and investors from all over the world to Northern Thailand. The aim was to achieve international attention; but with hindsight we can say that the government got more than it bargained for. Because this meeting took place some months after the protest meetings in Seattle in November 1999, activists not only from Thailand, but also from Asia and Europe and the US also went to the Chiang Mai meeting. Huge demonstrations were held (for some hours the demonstrators managed to seal off the hotel that was the venue for the meeting), but even more important, activists networked, and as a result the local activists from Klong Dan and their leaders, about two hundred in number, were introduced to international NGOs such as the NGO Forum on ADB, Environmental Defence and the Washington DC-based Bank Information Center. The locus for what was to become the largest international campaign against an ADB project was therefore the ADB's own annual meeting. It is an interesting paradox of the politics of multilateral institutions that a structure established at one point in time in order to serve one specific purpose (in this case networking between government officials, bankers and investors) at a later point in time became both a public relations rallying point and an important venue for networking for groups and individuals opposed to the prevailing order of multilateral institutions. Politics is full of contradictions and these provide the analyst with a valuable means of penetrating a certain issue-area.

Another issue that this case highlights is the enormous difference in worldview between that of multilateral institutions and of activists. One of the authors of this book (Morten Bøås) has attended a number of meetings between the ADB and leaders of the Klong Dan community, which clearly indicate how strikingly different are their interpretations of reality. The local residents are naturally concerned with Klong Dan and their local community, and they argue their case from this vantage point. Their main, and perhaps only, aim is to reclaim their way of life. This is an argument that an institution like the ADB is ill-equipped to deal with, and even to understand. In all these meetings, the ADB staff argued about the need for wastewater treatment of the more than 600,000 people who live in the greater Samut Prakarn region. Most would recognise the importance of this objective – except perhaps the Klong Dan community, for they consider that the ADB project, if located in Klong Dan, will destroy their livelihood. The trade-offs on behalf of the greater common good for which the ADB staff argue are of little interest, or even meaning, for the local residents. The result is two different worldviews that are not easily reconciled. For the NGO communities and the local residents the case seems to be completely clear: if a project has negative consequences, then the project should not be carried out. One might interpret such an argument as being against development, or at least in line with a certain dominant worldview which has been characterised as 'post-development'. The perspective of the ADB, on the other hand, with arguments about trade-offs between local communities and the greater common good, might be described as 'modernisation from above'.[26] It is highly questionable whether these very different perspectives can be reconciled at all, but this will clearly be an important issue in policy debate and the politics of multilateral institutions in the years to come.

We should also note that the Samut Prakarn case has set in motion a heated internal debate in the ADB pitting reformers against traditionalists. At the centre of this debate is the question of how to make the Inspection Panel function work better for all parties concerned. Suggestions are being put forward about making it more practical and less legalistic. This includes making it possible for local communities to file claims for inspection in their own language (presently, they must be in English). Another suggestion that has been proposed is to reorient the Inspection Panel function to an Ombudsman approach. If such initiatives are taken in the ADB it is likely that they will generate similar debates in other multilateral institutions. A number of NGOs are following this debate very closely, and they will almost certainly try to introduce it into other institutions as well. This is another example of the increasing power of NGOs, and raises the important question of the role and legitimacy of NGOs, to which we now turn.

LEGITIMACY AND REPRESENTATION – A CASE FOR CRITICAL ENGAGEMENT?

As we have seen earlier in this chapter, the internationalisation of the Pelosi Amendment was a major victory for the US NGO community. However, this event did not necessarily improve the relationship of the NGOs with the multilateral institutions. Many are still convinced that multilateral institutions are basically unreliable, and are inclined to distrust any activity by multilateral institutions until it has been thoroughly investigated and checked by outsiders. During the 1990s, the strategy of NGOs has been to increase their pressure on multilateral institutions to implement new policies and guidelines, to install independent monitoring bodies, and to become more transparent and open with information. Any concessions that were made by multilateral institutions were received critically, with requests for further guarantees and procedures. The process gained a momentum of its own: with multilateral institution documents paying increased attention to a particular issue-area, followed by NGOs pressing for even more concern and attention. This was particularly evident within the field of environmental issues. But in the process, it seems as if the US-based NGOs forgot that the development agenda was much more comprehensive than imposing environmental issues through a legalistic approach. The question is, why did this happen? If we return to the relationship between the NGOs and the United States, some underlying causes become evident.

Turning the financial instrument against multilateral institutions: the case of the World Bank

Over the years, US-based NGOs have on several occasions turned the financial instrument against the World Bank by requesting that Congress make funding for the World Bank's Independent Development Association (IDA) available only on very strict conditions. In 1992 and 1993, they carried out a major campaign against the tenth IDA replenishment. And, in 1992, they also objected strongly to the so-called 'Earth Increment' (additional World Bank funding for environmental purposes). They criticised it as a vague and useless concept. Lori Udall of the Environmental Defence Fund (EDF) argued: 'Sources close to the Bank revealed that the Earth Increment was a fund-raising ploy to ensure full IDA replenishment, rather than a genuine attempt to increase environmental lending' (quoted in Kolk 1996: 273). Partly owing to the NGO campaign, but also to a generally more adverse attitude toward the provision of additional financial resources, the major donors refused to honour the World Bank's request for *ad hoc* environmental funds.

At the heart of the IDA-10 Campaign was the Narmada Dam project in India,[27] and in particular the decision taken by the Board of the World Bank on 23 October 1992 to continue with the project, despite the objections of six EDs from important member countries (who together controlled 42 per cent of the total votes).[28] For the NGOs involved, the World Bank's handling of the Narmada project had seriously undermined its credibility, and their belief in the Bank's ability to generate reform on its own. The emerging consensus was that the World Bank had to be forced to reform; it would never do so voluntarily. The main means to enable NGOs to force reforms from the Bank was seen as an attack on its financial base; in other words, the funding the Bank received from its member countries, and particularly the major donor countries. A group of Indian, other Asian, and American NGOs which were part of the Narmada campaign launched an international campaign to oppose US$18 billion for the IDA-10 replenishment:

> The campaign called for the direction of IDA money to other multilateral and bilateral institutions that are more accountable, democratic and participatory. Because Narmada was symbolic of many of the institutional problems and policy violations widespread inside the Bank, NGOs felt that if the Bank could not address critical issues in such a high-profile problem project, then reform in other projects and programs was unlikely. They also felt that problems in the review of Narmada underscored the need for a permanent appeals mechanism to independently investigate problem projects. (Udall 2000: 401)

Speaking at a hearing of the House Subcommittee on Appropriations, Bruce Rich of the EDF argued:

> We strongly urge the Subcommittee to withhold all funding from the Bank until it has fully demonstrated in its operations, not in its rhetoric or policy proclamations, that project quality and environmental and social sustainability are the top priorities, and until it has totally reformed its restrictive policies concerning access to information by those affected by its projects as well as the public in general. (Rich 1993: 10)

In January 1993, 140 organisations from 20 countries, including borrowing countries, issued a statement to this end. However, although African and European NGOs – developmental as well as environmental – were generally united in their criticism of the World Bank, many expressed strong concern about putting budgetary pressure on the World Bank and other multilateral institutions that might affect the broader agenda of development assistance. The negative reaction from African NGOs to demands to withhold IDA funds led the American NGOs to moderate their position, attaching instead a number of conditions to the appropriation. Subsequently, in October 1993, the US Congress decided to approve IDA funds for two years instead of the standard three, and reduced the 1994 pledge by US$200 million. This self-imposed limit was linked to a request for increased information and the creation of an appeals commission.[29]

In the early 1990s, the adverse responses from European and, in particular, African NGOs had some impact on American NGOs concerned with multilateral institutions. They were more cautious when the issue of the Global Environment Facility (GEF) emerged. And when the House of Representatives discussed budget cuts in May 1994, NGOs such as Conservation International, Friends of the Earth and the National Resources Defence Council refused to support the Republican proposal for cuts in funding. The EDF, although not supporting the proposal, permitted the Republicans to make use of the EDF's arguments against the GEF.[30] Nevertheless, this response showed a change of heart compared to the approach they took before the restructuring of the GEF, when the most radical NGOs lobbied the US government to withhold all funds unless reforms were undertaken. This more moderate and engaged approach was, however, relatively short-lived, and rather than simply trying to decrease funding for the IDA and the GEF, a growing number of NGOs started to argue for the closure of the World Bank.[31] As the fiftieth anniversary of the Bretton Woods institutions came closer, more American NGOs began to support this idea in public. They created a specific campaign for the event under the banner 'Fifty Years is Enough', which was meant to imply that it was not reform that was required, but fundamental structural changes in these institutions.[32] The campaign put forward proposals such as removing the IDA from World Bank management and delinking the GEF from the World Bank. Some NGOs from other countries joined the campaign, but European NGOs in general did not at this stage support these proposals. In 1994 they were viewed as too extreme.

At the Annual Meeting of the World Bank and the IMF in October 1994 in Madrid, the division between the 'radical' and more moderate and accommodating NGOs became even more apparent. The groups that stressed the 'Fifty Years is Enough' theme attracted almost all public attention, leaving little room for other positions and points of view. The Madrid Declaration of the NGO Alternative Forum, which called unconditionally for the closure of the Bretton Woods institutions, exemplifies this more extreme position:

It is now time to put an end to the existence of these institutions. The only thing that now needs to be discussed is the schedule and social control in dismantling the Bretton Woods institutions. This process must be initiated with the immediate reduction in their funding. It is urgent to refuse every demand to enlarge IDA-11. These programs, currently administered by the World Bank group, must be put under immediate control of other institutions, to facilitate a rapid reorientation of their management. (Madrid Declaration of the Alternative Forum 1994: 1)

As the pressure continued, both from NGOs and some donor member countries, the World Bank adopted a more offensive strategy. With respect to the NGOs, it singled out its most radical opponents, arguing that these NGOs (mostly from the United States) had very limited understanding of the complex processes of development; that they cared only about the environment, not about people and their right to development. The NGOs singled out in this way replied that this was simply a World Bank effort to discredit them and their work, and was clearly related to their campaigns against funding for the Bank. Although this may well be true, even some of the more 'progressive' donor member countries in the Bank – such as the so-called 'like-minded countries' – started to express similar views. For instance, the Dutch ED remarked that the NGO lobbying had resulted in the requirement of EIAs, but not of assessment of a project's impact on poor people (see Kolk 1996). To a certain degree, it therefore seems that the radical protest during the Madrid meeting temporarily strengthened the World Bank position *vis-à-vis* its most radical critics. This was simply because the criticisms expressed by the Alternative Forum Declaration were way beyond what even the most 'progressive' donor member country in the Bank would agree with. Many countries had been supportive of arguments that the Bank (and other multilateral institutions) needed to pay much more attention to the environment and other emerging issue-areas such as gender and local participation. But these member countries wanted to reform the Bank from within; suggestions for closure were way outside their agenda. Another outcome of this was a rift in the NGO community. The more moderate ones, and in particular the operational NGOs, feared that they would lose the influence they had acquired over the years through consultation and involvement in World Bank projects.

Dilemmas and contradictions of NGO involvement

Although US NGOs in principle opposed conditionalities on aid, their campaigns clearly contributed to increasing it – in the interests (mainly) of protecting the environment. This conditionality also entailed a further centralization of power in the relationship between the Bank and borrowing countries, and perhaps within the Bank itself. These are examples of some of the dilemmas and contradictions that follow when NGOs become significant political actors in the multilateral system. This can have unintended and often perverse effects, such as opting out by powerful countries like India, a reduction in the volume of aid, and the increased power of the US. These may be briefly elaborated on.

The US NGOs' exclusive focus on the MDBs, and the World Bank in particular, is manifested in the establishment of inspection panels. The opportunity to file complaints against individual projects in order to increase World Bank accountability may well be a desirable aim in itself, but there are limits to what can be achieved through this approach. If such a complaint is filed, a borrower may be able to ignore it by simply dropping the loan request and seeking other sources of funds.[33] Many of the world's middle- and even low-income countries (but not the least developed countries) can rely increasingly on world capital markets, and can therefore choose less demanding lending instruments than those offered by multilateral institutions. In short, they can choose not to meet World Bank requirements and environmental conditionalities. For the NGO community, and in particular the NGOs from rich countries, this contradictory tendency should surely be disturbing. Their campaign for better environmental procedures in multilateral institutions might end up being ineffectual because private investors and financiers will almost certainly not apply the strict environmental conditionalities that multilateral institutions use today.

Another concern, related to the activity of US NGOs in particular, is the potential impact on donors' willingness to replenish development funds in the multilateral system. In particular, the budget cuts by the United States, which to some extent were legitimised by some NGOs, have posed a major challenge. In 1995, the World Bank even started an advertising campaign in major US newspapers trying to convince American taxpayers about the value of its work and the benefits to the US economy in terms of jobs and contracts.[33] US doubts about foreign aid were strengthened by the congressional Republican majority from 1995 and beyond, but other donor countries also worried about the quality and effectiveness of the project portfolio of multilateral institutions. Within a context in OECD countries of more carefully weighing the costs and benefits of foreign aid, it was unlikely that money saved on, say, IDA contributions would be used for bilateral or other forms of multilateral aid. Thus, the NGO campaign punished the World Bank, and perhaps reduced potential negative effects of IDA projects, but the overall effect of the campaign was to reduce levels of official development assistance (ODA). The provocative question that therefore arises is whether this process really benefited the less-developed countries; if not, whose interests did these cuts actually serve: the people in the less developed countries, the NGOs, or the Republicans in the US Congress who suddenly achieved a new source of legitimacy for their anti-aid campaign? One may argue that reduced ODA would save developing countries from future indebtedness, and from ill-conceived development projects, but this is equivalent to rejecting all ODA, and that is not the position of most people involved in the NGO community.

The NGO campaign against the World Bank has been dominated by *American* NGOs – because the World Bank is based in Washington DC, these NGOs have access to US decision makers, and the United States occupies a crucial position as the major donor. In the early 1990s, US NGOs tried to forge alliances with European and Southern NGOs, but it was the US NGOs that drove the debate forward and made the crucial decisions on strategy and tactics. In this period, non-American NGOs often expressed differing viewpoints, which made it difficult to keep the alliance together – the case of IDA replenishment being one obvious case. The MDB campaign in general, and the IDA replenishment campaign in particular, illustrate the tendency of US NGOs in this period to focus narrowly on the attainment of their specific objectives. The Republican anti-aid attitude and hostility toward multilateral institutions in general could easily be translated into budget reductions for MDBs under the pretext of environmental protection, open access to information, or the creation of an independent inspection function. What the US NGOs failed to see was that apart from some short-term common interests, their objectives differed enormously from those of the Republican majority in the US Congress. It is therefore quite possible to argue that it was in fact the Republicans who used the NGOs and not *vice versa*. It was Republican interests that were served by the cuts in ODA, and they were able to give their anti-aid campaign environmental credibility. The NGOs were not able to separate short-term from long-term interests, and this led them into an 'unholy alliance' with the anti-aid campaign of the Republican majority in Congress, which led to unintended and perverse effects. It is not easy to see why some NGOs seemingly lost track of their own agenda in this way, but it is instructive to observe the nature of the NGO two-level bargaining process. They must first use their bargaining leverage to gain access to the decision-making process. In these particular cases the easiest route to access and influence was through the legislative process at the national level, into which they were dragged. However, their experience here suggests that they did not realise that access to power is a double-edged sword.

We should keep in mind that the events described here took place in a certain historic period when NGOs still had to struggle for information and access to decision makers in multilateral institutions. However, the underlying problematic here is more than just a question of who is using whom for what purpose. It is even more a question about whose development we are talking about – and who speaks for them. It is to this question that we now turn.

Representation and legitimacy

Development means many different things to different people. As we noted with regard to the Samut Prakarn case, there are often differing worldviews which clash – most evidently when staff from multilateral institutions and activists discuss specific cases; they do not seem to be able to agree on anything at all, but speak past each other, with little regard or understanding for each other's arguments. Such disagreements occur at different levels. At the most general level, there are doubts about the 'development' objective itself: of modernisation and economic growth. At the next, there is a rejection of an 'engineering' approach to development (see Chapter 3) and doubts about the ability of multilateral institutions to deliver on their promises, over several decades, of abolishing poverty and achieving development. These institutions have increasingly been seen not as the solution, but part of the problem. Related, though conceptually separate, is a rejection of top-down, centralised processes of decision making. Such questions have been raised for decades, but they have gained a new urgency in recent years, largely owing to the role of NGOs, in a process which started with the early reformist approach of environmental NGOs in the early 1980s, and developed into a more holistic, but also more radical activist movement in the late 1990s/early 2000s. As pointed out by Pieterse (2001: 9) 'Development thinking and policy, then, is a terrain of hegemony and counter-hegemony.' Recent events gave more real political force to the 'counter-hegemonic' forces that many NGOs represent.

According to the Focus on the Global South NGO, good governance implies publicly accountable systems of rights, entitlements, laws, rules, distribution and use of resources, and decision making that is based on universal principles of equality, equity and justice, but which at the same time allows for the cultural specificities of a society or nation. This NGO sees the ADB's governance approach as the complete opposite, and a manifestation of its particular approach to development policy (see Focus on the Global South 2002):

> The ADB is a market fundamentalist in its economic and development approaches. Its poverty reduction strategy is based on unshakable beliefs in the wonders of rapid economic growth, financial liberalisation, privatisation, deregulation and increased market openness. By adding the phrase pro-poor growth to its usual range of operations, it seeks to justify its efforts towards private sector and market expansion. (Guttal 2002: 3–4)

This is just one example of the view increasingly expressed by NGOs that attempts to reform multilateral institutions over more than two decades have failed; that such an approach is fruitless. This has given rise to the phenomenon which we refer to as the 'politics of protest'. However, before we turn to this issue we need to address questions of representation and legitimacy, which relate to the question 'development for whom and for what purpose?'

We begin with the question of representation. A formal distinction is made in political science between functional and territorial representation; the latter attached to nation-states and the former to organisations. In these terms, NGOs may occupy an anomalous position, since they cannot normally claim to represent, on a territorial-wide basis, populations as such. The question arises, who do they represent? What constitutes their constituency: the staff of the NGO, its financial contributors, or the poor (either unspecified or at a specific location)? NGOs have not been able to offer credible answers to these questions, and many governments have used precisely such arguments when confronted with criticism from NGOs. But the question of representation is not easy for many governments either. The democratic credentials of many governments are anything but high. For this reason, NGOs often a have much higher level of legitimacy than the state, resulting in a somewhat paradoxical situation which may be summed up in the following way (see Table 4.4).

Table 4.4   Representation and legitimacy

	States	NGOs
Legitimacy	Low	High
Representativity	High	Low

This is, of course, to oversimplify the matter. For in concrete situations, the question is not only 'who do the NGOs represent?', but also 'are they competent – politically and technically – to make necessary trade-offs between the interests of different groups?' This additional point is well exemplified by the Samut Prakarn case. Here, influential NGOs like the NGO Forum on ADB, Environmental Defence and the Bank Information Center choose to speak for the inhabitants of Klong Dan, a small Thai community dependent on marine resources for its way of life. This is perfectly legitimate. But the question remains: what about the other 600,000 people who live in the Samut Prakarn region? They are urgently in need of wastewater treatment systems, and such facilities must be located somewhere. The inability or unwillingness of the NGO in this case even to acknowledge this problem is something we see as a weakness of its case. To extend this argument to the wider sphere, as NGOs begin to achieve real political power, they are also bound to face up to the challenges that this brings with it – of resolving conflicting, legitimate interests. This also implies that NGOs become a part of the research agenda for those who study the politics of the development system, and their words and deeds should be viewed with the same sort of engaged criticism as that which we direct towards multilateral institutions. Our perspective of critical engagement is not solely directed to multilateral institutions, but also to the politics around these institutions.

THE POLITICS OF PROTEST

Increased dissatisfaction with multilateral institutions is not necessarily limited to what is perceived as their 'top-down' and 'technocratic' approach, but is also often aimed at the neoliberal agenda which they are seen as promoting. Such criticisms, and the demands for closure of the IMF and the World Bank which accompany them, are at the heart of the new 'politics of protest'. The annual meetings of multilateral institutions, and even small-scale meetings of such institutions, have become rallying points for manifestations of resistance against these institutions and the policies and ideologies they are seen to represent.[35] This trend, if we can use such a word, started with the 'Fifty Years Is Enough' campaign against the World Bank and the IMF in 1994 (Fox and Brown 2000b), and culminated (perhaps) with the killing of Carlo Giuliani on the streets of Genoa by the Italian police on 20 July 2001. It is unclear whether we in the foreseeable future will see such levels of mass demonstrations (and violence), but Annual Meetings will surely continue to be an articulation of resistance and therefore also an integrated part of the politics of multilateral institutions. What are the characteristics of the politics of protest?

First, we should acknowledge that the politics of protest is born out of deep frustration and dissatisfaction with how multilateral institutions work. For those who articulate the politics of protest, these institutions are not a part of the solution, but a fundamental part of the problem. Reform is not possible, therefore the alternative is closure, particularly of institutions such as the World Bank and the IMF.[36] As regards the alternative to these institutions, those who voice this argument are divided into several camps. Some still have faith in multilateral institutions as such, and argue for a transfer of resources to the UN system; some would like to design new institutions; others offer no institutional solution but see this as a part of a greater revolutionary struggle.

Second, we should note that the nature and logic of the politics of protest has important traits of both autonomy and transnationalism. It is autonomous to the degree that both leaders and structures are in flux; they are more often temporary than permanent. Thus, people may participate actively in one or many organisations, or they can belong to none in particular. And the 'movement' itself is characterised by its transitional character; structures are established for the purpose of the event, not for permanency. The other main feature is the transnational character of the politics of protest. By transnational here we mean that it cuts through state borders without any connection to the state and its apparatus at large. Rather, a cobweb of relations binds together activists from all over the world through web-pages and listservers. The Internet is an important facilitator of exchange, but not the cause as such. Also, these transnational alliances and contact points are transitional to the degree that they are utilised according to circumstance and opportunity. Some may be quite involved in the preparatory phase of an event, but themselves be unable to come to the actual event; whereas others cross continents and regional borders in order to take part in such expressions of resistance. (The meeting between the Klong Dan activists and the representatives of international NGOs took place during the 2000 ADB Annual Meeting.) Finally, the autonomous and transitional character of the politics of protest provides the ground for not one agenda, but many – some of them contradictory in traditional political terms. But what a traditional political science approach fails to grasp is that people and groups come together as one for the specific event and because they need each other. The main strength in a mass rally is not, for example, protection against police brutality, but that it attracts much more media attention than any of the individual groups, or issues, could hope to achieve on their own. This is why we see activists for labour, environment, gender, gay rights and so on marching together. This has proved to be a potent force for criticism. It remains to be seen where it will lead.

POLICY MAKING IN MULTILATERAL INSTITUTIONS –
THE ART OF THE STATE?

The politics of multilateral institutions is not easily penetrated. The political processes within them may seem confusing and incoherent to outside observers, but they may perhaps be understood as iterated exercises of social practice. In order to make sense of what is going on we should take as a point of departure that policy outcomes are determined through interaction between three main sets of actors: member states, the multilateral institution itself and NGOs/civil societies. One of our basic points is that the fine art of multilateral policy making is no longer the prerogative of the state but rather that the field of politics in multilateral institutions is socially constructed through continuous interaction among the above mentioned set of actors. In this chapter we have shown how new actors have emerged within this field. Today there are non-state actors firmly established which neither the member states nor multilateral institutions dare to ignore. The costs are simply too high. As we have seen, it was the breakthrough on environmental issues that offered non-state actors their first path to influence in multilateral institutions. It was environmental issues that first opened up the World Bank to NGOs, and we have seen how this process has later repeated itself in organisations as diverse as the ADB and the WTO. This is an interesting pattern that we should certainly be aware of when we are trying to make sense of political processes in multilateral institutions.

Another important issue is the need to 'unpack the black boxes'. We cannot treat multilateral institutions as unilateral actors. As the case studies and illustrations have underscored, these are not monolithic organisations. All policy outcomes in multilateral institutions are the result of long and complicated internal processes influenced both by member states and NGOs and by the diverse historical experiences of the institutions concerned. Also, these are not static entities, but dynamic social institutions. Policies once adopted are not written in stone, but constantly open to adaptation, distortion and negotiation based on new experiences and competing interpretations of the reality one is faced with. As we have seen from some of the cases discussed in this chapter, there are often enormous differences between the worldview of multilateral institutions and that of social activists. Reality is always open to interpretation, and competing interpretations of reality surely place their mark on the politics of multilateral institutions.

Another important point emerging from this chapter is that of inter-institutional rivalry. The case study of how interaction between the World Bank and the UNDP contributed to redefining the UNDP's governance agenda is only one example of this within the system of multilateral institutions. As elsewhere, resources are scarce, and as a consequence the actors involved (that is, multilateral institutions) are competing for attention from potential donors and try to make themselves as attractive as possible by adapting their agendas according to the latest fads in development.

Finally, we should stress that even though we are very concerned about the role of the US in multilateral institutions, one cannot explain policy outcomes solely by reference to the US and its Treasury Department. As the different cases and illustrations have shown, there is much more to the politics of multilateral institutions. Ultimately, the most important reason for studying multilateral institutions is the importance they have for the well-being of millions of people. This is why we devote the next and final chapter of this book to the future of multilateral institutions.

5
The Future of
Multilateral Institutions

The multilateral institutions have in recent years been the focus of much critical and sometimes heated debate, with the World Bank often at the centre. But although the controversy around multilateral institutions has never been higher, the level of knowledge and informed criticism is not comparably high. In this concluding chapter we shall critically review the situation and prospects for change, not only for the World Bank but also other multilateral institutions discussed in this book. Unlike some others, we do not favour closure of the World Bank – but we do see the need for substantive reform, for reasons that we shall argue. The Bank is only a component, albeit a significant component, of the multilateral system. What happens to this institution will depend on what happens to the others – and to the global economic and political system as a whole.

The forces towards continued and increasing globalisation – with regard to the movement of goods and services, and of capital (if not of labour) – are powerful. The tasks of the World Trade Organisation and the International Monetary Fund are intimately associated with these two dimensions of global flows. But the multilateral system is fragile. In a sense, the challenge of the WTO and the IMF is to make globalisation work. But the World Bank and the UN agencies (and, to more varying extents, the regional development banks) are concerned more specifically with development. Their challenge, one might say, is to make globalisation work for the poor.

A crucial determinant for the future of the multilateral institutions will therefore be the future of globalisation. Conversely, continued globalisation is dependent on these institutions; the WTO and the IMF – to a greater extent than the others – will influence how this future plays out. The international system will continue to be a market system, but it remains to be seen whether the neoliberal ideology associated with this system, and so

influential in multilateral institutions in the 1980s, will wax or
wane. Will the World Bank, for example, through its policies and
programmes, be promoting or seeking to modify the impact of
market forces?

In assessing the future of the multilateral institutions we should
be aware of certain significant trends. One is what might be called
the privatisation of the multilateral system. Partnership with
business and industry is much discussed today, both in the UN
system through Kofi Annan's 'Global Compact' initiative, and in
the World Bank and the regional development banks. Will we in
the future be confronted by a much more thoroughgoing involvement of private actors in the multilateral system than that implied
by the still rather limited flows of private funds that we can observe
today? What implications will such developments have for new
issue-areas and linkages in the early twenty-first century, and for
the organisation of multilateral institutions? And how will this
relate to neoliberalism? Will increased privatisation strengthen it
or will some new version of social corporatism take its place?

Another issue that we raise in this final chapter is the role of civil
society engagement with multilateral institutions and the mass
protest that has followed. Is the politics of protest just a passing
fad? If it has a lasting influence, will this result in a wholly new
approach for some – or even all – of the multilateral institutions?

Regionalisation may also become a major issue for the future of
multilateral institutions. This issue can become salient in at least
two different but related ways. Regional country groups based on
some sort of regional identity may become more important in
the politics of multilateral institutions in the future. Related to
this is the fact that regional approaches to development are a new
trend. The regional development banks are increasingly taking on
the role as 'regionalising actors', while other multilateral institutions channel more resources than previously through regional
arrangements.

What will be the combined impact of these different influences
on the balance of power between the multilateral institutions? It
is the member states – both lenders and borrowers – that have the
power to determine this; what role will they play in bringing about
change? Before we turn to these specific issues we will try to clarify
our general position on multilateralism and the case for profound
reform of multilateral institutions.

REVOLUTION, REFORM OR COSMETIC CHANGE?

Some see the World Bank as the solution to poverty and environmental degradation, whereas for others it is not the solution, but
a central part of the problem. In broad terms, those engaged in
public debate about the World Bank can be divided into three
camps: those who favour closure, those who advocate profound
reform, and those who propose incremental adaptation to new circumstances. The two extreme camps rarely speak to each other,
but we belong to the second, and feel the need to argue our case
in relation to both of the others, especially, given our critical views,
in relation to the argument for closure. We are in favour of multilateralism, multilateral solutions and multilateral institutions. This
does not mean that we agree with current thinking in multilateral
institutions. So why do we still argue for reform and not closure?
The reason is simply that we live in an imperfect world, which will
not be improved simply by closing the World Bank and other multilateral institutions. This would, rather, make the situation even
worse for the poorer and weaker countries. The alternatives to multilateralism are bilateralism and unilateralism. In current
circumstances, it would in practice be 'uni-Americanism'. We refer
back to the brief theoretical elaboration in Chapter 1, where we
outlined our critical approach to multilateralism. Multilateral institutions are seen as co-evolving in a reciprocal relationship with
global structural change. Multilateralism is about the establishment of social order in a changing world, an order which emerges
from the nexus between material conditions, interests and ideas.
The outcome is not simply the result of naked power and self-
interest of competing national states. These states operate within
a social order of their own, mutual, construction. The current international social order is broadly neoliberalist, based on the market
but also on agreed rules maintained by institutions. The international order is thus stabilised and perpetuated through
'institutionalisation'. The multilateral institutions do reflect power
relations in the global political economy, and they facilitate
worldviews and beliefs in accordance with these power relations.
However, as Chapter 4 has demonstrated, the politics of multilateral institutions are complex, and outcomes are not simply
determined by the distribution of power between the individual
member states. They are influenced also by non-state actors, and

the staff of the multilateral institutions themselves affect how choices are framed and outcomes reached. Several case studies and observations in this book have revealed the considerable extent to which multilateral institutions are social institutions. Multilateralism is social practice. This is necessarily an iterative process, which creates webs of norms which entangle the very actors that create them. Our point is that multilateral institutions possess a clear coercive quality, and actors who enter into multilateral processes are necessarily changed by them – however powerful they may be. Herein lies also the power of multilateralism as a protection for the weak against the strong. For in its webs and entanglements the strongest country also is bound, albeit to a lesser degree. Otherwise the whole multilateral order will be broken. Thus, although the role of the United States is crucial for our understanding of the World Bank and its policies, as we have also shown we cannot explain policy outcomes solely by reference to them. There is far more to the politics of multilateral institutions. Multilateral institutions can surely be used by powerful states as part of a hegemonic strategy; but they also serve the interests of the weak. This is why we, in an imperfect world, argue and work for substantial reform of multilateral institutions, including the World Bank.[1] If the World Bank were to be closed, this would in all probability lead not merely to much lower levels of official development assistance (ODA), but also lower levels of investment and trade in poorer countries. The closure argument is in our view misplaced. But what is required is more than mere cosmetic change, or incremental adaptation to changing circumstances. A substantial reform of multilateral institutions, in a direction which better protects the interests of the poor, is needed. Whether this occurs will depend on the outcome of some major interrelated trends. We will, in this remainder of this chapter, outline those which we see as most important, beginning with the increased infusion of private money in multilateral institutions.

THE PRIVATISATION OF MULTILATERAL INSTITUTIONS

One of the most significant changes in the multilateral system over the last years is the increased participation of the private sector. Interaction between multilateral institutions and the private sector is not new. However, over the past decade there has been an increase in the scale and impact of this interaction. New forms of cooperation have emerged, ranging from global, multi-stakeholder initiatives to operational partnerships in individual countries and communities.[2]

One example of the former is Kofi Annan's 'Global Compact'. The formal objective of this initiative is to engage the private sector to work with the UN, in partnership with labour and NGOs, to promote good corporate practices based on nine principles drawn from the Universal Declaration of Human Rights, the ILO's Fundamental Principles and Rights at Work and the Rio Declaration on Environment and Development.[3] Companies are challenged to move toward good corporate practices as understood by the broader international community, rather than relying on their often superior bargaining position *vis-à-vis* national governments, particularly in small and poor countries (Ruggie 2001). This initiative has been praised in mainstream newspapers; for example, the *Washington Post* described it as the 'most creative reinvention of the UN yet'. But it has been criticised by NGOs such as CorpWatch: 'the UN's positive image is vulnerable to being sullied by corporate criminals, while companies get a chance to "bluewash" their image by wrapping themselves in the flag of the United Nations' (Transnational Resource and Action Center 2000: 2). As so often with respect to multilateral institutions, views differ widely. One side sees laudable innovation, whereas the other side sees a process that is seriously flawed and potentially destructive.

Different people and groups disagree about where this development may lead us, but few question that the recent wave of private sector participation is characterised both by a quantitative increase in joint projects and initiatives, and also by the proliferation of new mechanisms for private sector participation. A recent UN report (UN 2001) distinguishes between five different forms of private sector interaction with multilateral institutions:

- *Policy dialogue* – this includes formal and informal participation of the private sector in official intergovernmental deliberations and in institutional governance. It involves a series of different measures ranging in scope and formality from full participation in a multilateral governing body (for example, in the Joint United Nations Programme on HIV/AIDS), participation in commissions, committees, task forces and working groups, to informal consultative mechanisms and global policy networks.

- *Advocacy* – these partnerships are cooperative initiatives between multilateral institutions and non-state actors to raise public awareness and support for multilateral institutions' objectives and programmes.
- *Mobilizing private funds* – this includes joint efforts by multilateral institutions and the private sector to mobilise public and private capital for development aid. It also includes initiatives aimed at facilitating private investment, rather than raising it directly (for example, the Investment Deliverables Initiative, which is a joint effort by the International Chamber of Commerce and the United Nations Conference on Trade and Development (UNCTAD)). It also includes partnerships to mobilise and establish philanthropic funds. Well-known examples of philanthropic contributions include the US$1 billion donation by Ted Turner to the United Nations and the Bill and Melinda Gates Foundation's US$750 million grant to the Global Alliance for Vaccination and Immunisation (GAVI).
- *Information and learning partnerships* – this includes joint efforts to share research and learning. The Global Compact is one example of such learning fora, another is the Business Partners for Development Programme – a global network consisting of about 120 companies, civil society organisations and government agencies – convened by the World Bank in 1998.
- *Operational delivery* – these are partnerships where the private sector partner plays a role in design, implementation and/or evaluation of projects/programmes on the ground. Examples include the Refugee Registration Project; a partnership between the United Nations High Commission on Refugees (UNHCR) and Microsoft and its corporate partners to improve information management in refugee crises, and an agreement between UNAIDS and Coca-Cola to channel the company's in-kind assistance, in particular with regard to logistics and marketing, to priority activities against AIDS in Africa.

As we have already mentioned, interaction between multilateral institutions and the private sector is not new. Several multilateral institutions have long traditions for such involvement.[4] However, there are currently many signs that the organisational structure of multilateral institutions is changing as a consequence of increased private sector participation. The aforementioned Ted Turner donation resulted, for example, in two organisational innovations: the United Nations Foundation (UNF), an independent not-for-profit organisation, run by an independent Board of Directors, and the United Nations Fund for International Partnerships (UNFIP), an autonomous trust fund operating under the leadership of the Deputy Secretary General, and including several senior executives of the Rockefeller Foundation and the Ford Foundation on its board.[5] Among other examples of organisational innovation we can mention the Division for Business Partnerships in the UNDP, the World Bank's Business Partnership and Outreach Group, the World Health Organisation's Private Partnership Unit, the UNHCR's Private Sector and Public Affairs Service and ILO's Management and Corporate Citizenship Programme. All of these institutions were established after 1995, most of them after 1999.

It is increasingly recognised by practitioners that such partnerships represent both opportunities and challenges. The UN states that:

> In short, non-state actors have become increasingly influential in the United Nations system, at the global, national and local levels. Although co-operation with such non-state actors raises its own set of strategic and practical challenges, it is increasingly necessary if the United Nations is to remain relevant and effective in meeting the real needs of people in today's world. At the same time, co-operation must be managed in a manner that does not compromise the independence and neutrality of the UN or its character as an organisation of Member States. (UN 2001: 7)

The recent increase in the number of partnerships may be the result of forces both from within multilateral institutions and from their external environment. Increased private sector participation is in part a consequence of scarce access to external finance. But it may also be a result of internal processes. As we have seen, over the last two decades, the neoliberal ideology which gives the private sector a core role in development has become the dominant worldview in multilateral institutions. Increasing the role of the private sector in one's own operations may be a way of 'practising what you preach'. It may also be a response to increased private sector interest in participating in the operations of multilateral institutions: which in turn may be motivated both by a desire to practice philanthropic values, and also to gain access to new business opportunities.

It is important to assess the possible ramifications of increased private sector participation for global governance. As research on traditional privatisation at the state level shows, it is a gross simplification to treat these processes as 'zero-sum games' (Bull 2002). Rather, these are processes in which the role and organisation of the public institutions involved are redefined. Instead of being hierarchical organisations, in which member states are the only actors with an official voice on policy,[6] multilateral institutions are thus increasingly taking the form of fragmented networks of governance that officially include both public and private actors. Thus, the multilateral system is becoming an arena for encounters between different forces rather than a system constituted mainly by state actors. What we are currently witnessing therefore is a pluralisation of governance structures (O'Brien et al. 2000). This trend raises a number of challenging questions both regarding the impact on operation of multilateral institutions, and concerning more general consequences for governance of multilateral institutions. Three questions in particular arise in assessing the likely impact of privatisation on multilateral institutions.

Will new partnerships lead to fragmentation of multilateral institutions? The new partnerships were introduced partly as a means of making multilateral institutions more efficient. According to the dominant economic paradigm, the private sector operates in a more goal-oriented and effective manner. However, the new partnerships have so far created a series of new units. If coordination is not strengthened, this increases the risk of fragmentation of the institutional structure and duplication of effort.

Will such partnerships lead to a lack of coherence in development efforts? Over the last years some sort of consensus has developed about what constitutes 'best practice' with regard to development policy. One part of this 'consensus' is that programming characterised by nationally managed, coordinated investments supported by multiple partners gives the best long-term effect on development. The 'fund mode', that most of the new partnerships operate under, challenges this 'programme mode', by focusing on quick disbursement linked to results. If not integrated in a coherent framework, they may weaken the coherence and long-term thinking of development efforts.

Will privatisation lead to a distortion of policy objectives? As pointed out by Cutler et al. (1999b), 'rules' established by private sector participants tend to favour some actors over others. Increased use of partnerships may also result in a distortion of development objectives. The choice of which projects to support may be determined largely by where there happen to be private sector partners and hence funding available. There is also a risk that sectors in which there are strong private sector interests may be given priority over sectors in which international firms have fewer stakes (for example, within the social field, the health sector may be favoured over education). Increased privatisation will also raise important questions concerning global governance, of which the following two are most pertinent.

How will the new partnerships affect the power of the bureaucracies of multilateral institutions? Here, there are contradictory signs. On the one hand their power may be diminishing because private actors are taking over a number of the functions of multilateral institutions. On the other hand, multilateral institutions may increase their power as they become the focal points in complex networks of governance. They may hence control large amounts of resources and – through their access to information and specialised knowledge – exert influence over policy making in many broad fields and indeed over the development agenda as a whole.[7]

How do the new partnerships affect developing-country influence? Particularly in the UN system, based as it is on the one-country/one-vote principle, concerns have been raised about possible distortion of the balance of power between OECD countries, in which most major business and private foundations are based, and developing countries which still have a relatively weak private sector. Increased private sector influence may weaken developing country influence in multilateral institutions.

We are not yet in a position to answer these questions, but we believe that private sector participation is one of the most important issues with regard to the future of multilateral institutions. This trend may be driven by, and also promote, more emphasis on neoliberal approaches. But this view may be based on an oversimplified interpretation of the relationship between state and market, and the nature of corporatism. In Scandinavia, and indeed much of Europe, social policy arrangements were based on corporatist arrangements between state and market, whereas the new social corporatism discussed in some parts of the multilateral systems is by contrast liberal, in the individualistic sense of the word. In the former model, the state grows out of, and in a sense is, the people. In the latter, arrangements grow out of initiatives by the liberal middle classes. Inclusion into such arrangements is voluntary and based on human rights of the individual. These policies are embedded in a neoliberal discourse which condemns 'old-fashioned' beliefs in a strong state. Rather, the role of the state is to create enabling environments for communities and businesses, facilitate the establishment of social security arrangements and enhance and monitor inclusionary processes. Public–private partnership is here the key formula. This way of reasoning has little to do with the welfare-state ideology, but it is related to earlier liberal thinking about a *social state*. The market is not an end in itself, but a device to meet needs. The product of this kind of thinking is a new liberal version of social corporatism.

Whichever model emerges, it is clear that a new, more nuanced view on the virtues of neoliberalism will have a major impact on how member countries and multilateral institutions deal with increased private sector participation. The new emphasis in the World Bank, the ADB and elsewhere on 'pro-poor growth' is both a manifestation of this way of thinking, and also an attempt by these institutions to confront the massive criticism they have received from civil societies. According to Braathen (2000), the 2001 *World Development Report, Attacking Poverty*, is an example of such thinking in multilateral institutions. But the approach presented in this document may be criticised as an unhappy compromise between two very different positions, in response to attacks from civil society critics. In future, the fate of multilateral institutions will be closely linked to how successfully such critics, especially in major donor countries, are in their attempts to influence their respective governments.

CIVIL SOCIETY AND THE FUTURE OF
MULTILATERAL INSTITUTIONS

Activists marching together – in the name of labour, environment, women, gays or other groups and issues – have proved to be a potent critical force. The politics of protest thus manifested is born out of a deep frustration with how multilateral institutions work. For many of those who participate in social activism directed towards multilateral institutions, these institutions are not a part of the solution, but an integral part of the problem. Their criticism of the World Bank and its current president, James Wolfensohn, is therefore harsh. But these social activists are not Wolfensohn's only critics. There are also powerful opponents who think that Wolfensohn, the World Bank and other multilateral institutions have been much too forthcoming towards social activists from civil society organisations. Particularly in the United States, writers, researchers (mainly economists) and politicians from the right argued that Wolfensohn's attempts to make the World Bank friendlier to external constituencies, notably the NGOs, have made the institution soft-headed, less rigorous in their analysis, and hence less relevant. These critics argue that the World Bank has surrendered its intellectual integrity and sense of direction by embracing a string of new issue-areas regardless of their merit in relation to the World Bank's core mission, namely facilitating economic growth. Larry Summers, the former US Treasury secretary and current president of Harvard University, is one of the most prominent critics of the 'new' direction of the World Bank under Wolfensohn's presidency. According to Summers: 'there is little evidence that giving weight to local communities – in World Bank jargon, "empowerment" – resulted in improved decision making ... [and] that the move toward empowerment, rather than an economic approach is standing in some ways for a reduced emphasis on the analytical element in the bank's work' (Summers, quoted in Fidler 2001: 2). Echoing the statement of his predecessor, the US Treasury secretary, Paul O'Neill, has characterised the World Bank's work as excessively diffuse, and argued that the World Bank should focus strictly on projects that raise productivity and income levels. What these critics are afraid of is not that World Bank and other multilateral institutions' projects and policies will lead to environmental degradation, or harm to women and indigenous peoples; rather that much emphasis on what they see as the soft (social) sectors of development will result in the World Bank losing sight both of the need to undertake rigorous analysis and to support market forces. They want to protect what they see as the core of World Bank operations. These views are closely related to those underlying the report of the International Financial Institutions Advisory Commission. This commission was established by the US congress under the second Clinton administration. It was chaired by the Carnegie Mellon University economist Allan Meltzer. The main conclusion of the report was that the World Bank should scale back its functions and return to its basic objectives – facilitating economic growth. This report was seen by the right-wing opposition to the World Bank and Wolfensohn as a confirmation of their views, and it is no secret that these are shared by many influential actors in the Bush II administration, among them the Treasury secretary Paul O'Neill. Many of the participants on this side of the debate prefer unilateralism to multilateralism, both because they see financial institutions such as the World Bank as serving to distort market forces, and because they see multilateralism as a constraint on US foreign economic policy. To the degree that they support multilateral institutions such as the World Bank, it is as a useful instrument for projecting US influence on developing countries.

The World Bank and other multilateral institutions are therefore currently under attack from two sides. One wants to broaden the World Bank agenda and reduce the dominance of neoliberal economics, whereas the other wants to return to basic objectives and narrow the development agenda. The outcome of this process is highly uncertain. Much will depend on whether the current wave of social activism around multilateral institutions is sustained. An important issue in this regard is the level of violence associated with mass protest around international meetings. If sustained pressure on multilateral institutions is to maintain its momentum we believe it important that these demonstrations are massive but peaceful. We know from experience that violence is the responsibility not only of activists but also of the police; much could have been different both in Gothenburg and Genoa if the police had shown more restraint and opted for a more low-key profile. By 'securitising' the politics of protest, police forces have added fuel to the fire. As Buzan et al. (1988) put it, in their analysis of 'securitisation', security is a speech-act. But if protests against the World Bank and other multilateral institutions, and the momentum for reform and change that follow, are to be sustained, they have to be carried forward by a mass movement, and not by a small group of 'professional' street activists, accustomed to taking part in street fights with police forces. Otherwise the majority of (non-militant) activists will no longer take part in huge displays of opposition, and the current momentum for reform will suffer. It is for this reason that we view the events during the 2002 World Bank ABCDE conference in Oslo as so satisfactory (ABCDE stands for Annual Bank Conference on Development Economics). Whereas Norwegian media prepared in their headlines for the 'battle of Oslo', over 12,000 activists marched peacefully through the city (the largest such demonstration ever) and not a single window was broken. There are many reasons for this, but apparently both the police and the activists (even the so-called 'black bloc') learned from the mayhem of Gothenburg and Genoa. If this is the case, then it is good news for those who favour a critical engagement perspective aimed at far-reaching and substantial reform of multilateral institutions.

REGIONALISM AND MULTILATERAL INSTITUTIONS

Regionalisation is an important trend in the global political economy, and it is also putting its mark on the debate about the future role of multilateral institutions. At present, changes are perhaps most rapid in Europe. (As noted earlier in this book, this may lead to a more coherent EU approach to multilateralism as a counterweight to the United States.) But similar processes are also under way in other parts of the world, leading to coalitions between both lending and borrowing member states. The Association of South East Asian Nations (ASEAN) is one such example, [8] and it is noteworthy that in Japan public opinion favours the ADB much more than the World Bank. Our point is that regional identity seems to be in the process of becoming an important issue in the politics of multilateral institutions. This gives rise to tensions not only between the RDBs and global institutions but also within the RDBs themselves. One striking example is the African Development Bank (AfDB).

The principle for the distribution of resources in the AfDB is to approve at least one loan for each recipient member country in any given year, providing those members are not under sanctions due to their payment record. In this way the AfDB has attempted to counterbalance some of the prejudices of bilateral donors.[9] Thus, at face value there is no regional bias in the AfDB's lending processes. However, if we break down loan and grant allocations on a region-by-region pattern a different picture emerges. Then we find that North Africa is the largest receiver of non-concessional loans from the AfDB. The North African share of AfDB lending is partly balanced by their small share of soft money from the African Development Fund (ADF), but their dominance both with respect to the amount that they borrow and their relatively large share of the votes constitutes a continued source of tension in the AfDB. In 1995/96, when the AfDB's development fund ran out of money, the countries of North Africa obtained 85.9 per cent of total loans approved, while countries in the Central African region accounted for 11.8 per cent, countries in the Southern African region received 2 per cent, those in the Eastern African region 0.2 per cent and the Western African region 0.1 per cent (AfDB 1996). This lop-sided distribution does reflect the ability of the relatively more developed parts of the continent to absorb and service non-concessional debt, but it is also an illustration of a permanent point of tension in the AfDB. In fact, only the donor–recipient country cleavage seems to have been more important than the conflict between various regional groups over influence (voting power) and resources (percentages of loans and grants) (Bøås 2001a). The introduction of the AfDB's new credit policy which classified 39 of the AfDB's borrowing member countries as ineligible for non-concessional loans has exacerbated this trend.

Similar regional tensions, albeit on a lesser scale, can be identified in the other RDBs as well. This is one reason why the Asian Development Bank recently has made regionalisation one of its main priorities (see ADB 2002b). Another is to be found in the historical context of the Southeast Asia region, and how different historical experiences, different ideological heritages and different expectations among the policy elites have led to different conceptualisations of the idea of the region. One example is Australia's 'universal' regionalism as opposed to Singapore's and Malaysia's insistence on the specificities of an Asia that suits their domestic and international needs. Another example is the contrasting approaches from China and Japan. Japan's regional project is the result of indigenous economic developments and a conscious political strategy orchestrated jointly by government and the business elite. By contrast, the emerging Chinese 'commonwealth' has a much more open architecture. With respect to ASEAN, its establishment was originally a product of shared threat perceptions, but these were essentially inward-looking (see Acharya 1998). Formal intergovernmental projects have primarily been bulwarks of interstate political stability. Partly due to a range of potential conflicts and territorial disputes between the member countries, these projects have failed to spur economic growth and development and provide the post-Cold War security framework that the ADB is searching for.

The nature of the ADB's attempt to promote regionalisation has changed with the circumstances in the region. In the early days, the ADB coordinated studies on subregional projects and made financial contributions to regional research institutions. However, after the end of the Cold War, the ADB has strengthened its regional role, and has started to use its regional technical assistance programmes in a more active manner in order to support more diversified regional activities.

The ADB's renewed emphasis on regionalisation has focused in particular on the Greater Mekong Subregion (GMS), and the concept of growth triangles. The ADB has funded a comprehensive study of the prospects for increased economic cooperation and development among the six countries of the GMS: Cambodia, Lao PDR, Myanmar, Thailand, Vietnam and the Yunnan Province of China. With the assistance of the ADB, these countries entered into a programme of subregional economic cooperation in 1998.[10] The programme has essentially been pragmatic and activity-driven. The countries involved are supposed to collaborate on specific activities within the framework of existing relationships, and the programme does not aim at the creation of a trade bloc with time-bound objectives such as those under ASEAN. The other main part of the new regionalisation strategy of the ADB is the promotion of the concept of 'growth triangles', argued by Mitsuo Sato (former president of the ADB) to be 'a unique Asian solution to the operational problems of regional integration among countries at different stages of economic development and with different social and economic systems' (quoted in Thant et al. 1994: xiii). In both forms of regional engagement, the ADB plays a role as a facilitator and networker, conducting studies and bringing people together. As such, the ADB has become a regionalising actor – playing a strategic role in the promotion of regionalisation through three means. Through research and regional technical assistance, the ADB seeks to increase regional member countries' understanding of the importance of cooperation, identify possible bottlenecks to cooperation and suggest how these could be overcome. Second, acting as an 'honest broker', it seeks to encourage dialogue, suggesting approaches and identifying possible projects. Third, it not only provides funds from its own resources, but also helps to mobilise funds from other sources – bilateral and multilateral, and from the private sector.

Similar processes are also under way in the Inter-American Development Bank. Latin America as a region is often seen in terms of common language, history and culture, but regionalism in Latin America has its roots in two competing visions that continue to shape regional initiatives. These are on one hand Simon Bolivar's idea of a Spanish-American unity – a united Latin America in common front against the United States – and on the other hand, a US-initiated idea of the unity of the hemisphere, first expressed in the Monroe Doctrine of 1823. The IDB is itself a compromise between the Bolivarian dream and the Monroe Doctrine. It was first conceived of as a Latin American bank, but could not be established until US interests were incorporated. Soon after establishment, the IDB's first president Filipe Herrera declared 'We will be the Bank of integration' (Herrera 1974). In the 1960s, '70s and '80s, the IDB concentrated its regional activities on formal intergovernmental programmes and arrangements, but recently it has also shifted its attention to more flexible arrangements. Its main showcase in this regard is the Plan Puebla Panama. This regional scheme involves eight southern Mexican states,[11] Central America and Panama. The scheme is not directed toward formal integration between states, but rather to construct a new region – 'Meso-America' – through development projects facilitating transport, communications, and commercial and labour exchange. These are to be developed primarily by the private sector, but with governmental support and multilateral assistance (from the IDB and other multilateral institutions). One of the favourite IDB arguments has been that the cultural affinity and infrastructural similarity between the southern Mexican states and Central American countries will help promote this plan. However, this has also been the source of fierce opposition from social and labour groups which fear that the Plan Puebla Panama will create one large cheap labour pool at the service of the *maquiladora* industry, and at the expense of indigenous peoples and small-holding peasants.[12] The debate about a Bolivarian or a Monrovian vision on Latin American regionalism is still unresolved, and the IDB is currently, through initiatives such as the Plan Puebla Panama, in the middle of this debate. It has become a regionalising actor.

It is uncertain where processes of regionalisation will lead multilateral institutions in the future. However, we suspect that we will see more regional coordination of joint positions in global multilateral institutions such as the World Bank, the IMF and the WTO. The actual impact that national positions will have on a regional level is uncertain, but the possibility of more coherent EU and ASEAN positions on macro-policy issues in institutions such as the World Bank and the IMF may help to redress the current imbalance between the United States and other member countries. It could be a first step toward a more open debate about the virtues of neoliberalism; but this will also depend on the continued strength of civil society activism in European countries. It is only if pressured by these forces that European countries will start to genuinely question the dominant economic paradigm of multilateral institutions. Here we see the possibility for some interesting alliance building with Japan and the ASEAN countries, which still have a different view concerning the role of the state in development than that which dominates the debate in the US.

We are convinced that the RDBs' rediscovery of their regional role is more than just the latest development fad. They will stay on the regional scene, but as illustrated by the new approaches of the ADB and the IDB they will seek to fulfil their mandate through flexible arrangements in cooperation with both national governments, local governments and the private sector. The Plan Puebla Panama is yet another example of new partnerships between private sector actors and multilateral institutions. And it has already stimulated a reaction from civil society representatives in the region. This is a good demonstration of how interconnected are the three major trends which we have discussed in this chapter: privatisation, increased civil society involvement and regionalisation. What will be the combined effect of these, and other trends, and how should these be assessed from a perspective of 'critical engagement'?

CONCLUSION: CRITICAL ENGAGEMENT AND THE FUTURE OF MULTILATERAL INSTITUTIONS

As we have sought to show in this chapter, the multilateral institutions are subject to a variety of forces which will interact in the coming years. This will occur within a broad, and still changing post-Cold War context in which the tension between left and right is replaced by a tension between the global and the local, and between the market and civil society. Both private firms and NGOs will interact with the multilateral institutions in a complex set of relationships played out within a politicised arena, where issues of legitimacy and governance will increasingly come to the fore. And regional arrangements may also be seen as the ideal solution to the dilemma of global versus local, and the downplaying of the nation-state.

The outcome of these different forces will affect each institution differently, and hence the balance of power and division of labour between them. In broad terms, as we have shown, one may conceive of the set of institutions as comprising a spectrum: from the WTO, through the IMF, the World Bank and the RDBs, to the UN agencies. These will compete – for resources and influence – but also collaborate. But it is the nation-states, the member countries of the multilateral institutions that will – whether by determined action or by default – decide the fate of these institutions. And the United States will continue to be the most powerful state. It is therefore worth briefly examining the policy of this major player, in a world where, at least recently, we are seeing increased US unilateralism (uni-Americanism), dressed up as multilateralism.

There has always been a tension in US foreign policy between unilateralists and multilateralists, but since the late 1960s a number of analysts have stated that something loosely defined as *Pax America* has passed away. The view was that the United States had turned into a powerful, but 'ordinary country'.[13] The political implication was that the United States was in decline; it could no longer run the world the way it had been able to do before, but had to rely more heavily on multilateralism.

There was however a contrary argument, that the American 'empire' remained as secure as ever. For scholars such as Susan Strange, the new challenges that the United States faced from the 1960s did not decrease US structural power – the power that it enjoys through the dollar, through its military strength, and its lead in advanced technologies. All talk of decline was therefore nothing but a myth (see Strange 1982). Stephen Gill (1990) made similar arguments but from a different conceptual framework. According to Gill, the argument about US decline was built on false assumptions about how the global political economy worked. It did not take into consideration the shift that had taken place from a period of a competitive world political economy made up of nation-states to a globalised political economy where the distinction between the domestic and the international had been blurred by the transnationalisation of the world economy. The argument was that one could no longer conceive of hegemony in the form of the possessions of nation-states, but rather 'the developed practice of the international system as a whole' (Cox 2002: 57). Here, US structural power was seen as deriving from the English language, the size and the dynamism of the US economy, the US military apparatus and the multicultural nature of US society which mirrored the world in ways that other countries did not. Thus, in a world of transnational capital created by the United States, and in which US firms still played a dominant role, and the key economic players acted in accordance with the scripts written in Washington DC, the future for American hegemony looked very promising. Whatever the merits of these two views of the world, it was apparent during the Reagan and Clinton administrations that US foreign policy was balanced between unilateralism and multilateralism.

It was widely expected that US foreign policy under George Bush, Jr would move toward a more unilateral approach to foreign policy. Initially there were some signs that this was the case, but then came September 11 which profoundly altered US foreign policy. Some have argued that the US now seeks to enroll so many allies around its actions that it is practising multilateralism.[14] But multilateralism implies common decisions on issues based on generalised principles of conduct; multilateral diplomacy reduced to rallying support for decisions taken unilaterally is in essence a violation of multilateralism. This has been most evident in relation to military actions, but other actions of the Bush administration have given cause to question the US multilateral stance. Their unwillingness to ratify the Kyoto protocol is one example, but perhaps the most vivid case is the imposition of steel tariffs by the US in March 2002. The Bush administration argued that steel industries are given direct subsidies in other countries and therefore the tariffs are justified. However, under the multilateral order established by the United States itself, this is for the WTO to decide and not for the US unilaterally. Another example of the new unilateralism in US foreign policy is their demands to developing countries during the UN conference 'Financing for Development' in Monterrey, Mexico in April 2002. Here the US required that developing countries, in order to obtain loans and grants from multilateral institutions, would have to adhere to Western values and norms, such as multiparty elections and a market economy. And the US representatives also argued for more grants rather than loans. Both European representatives and those from developing countries were sceptical of the American proposals made in Monterrey.

The situation immediately following September 11 seems to be that the United States acts and then tells other countries to line up behind it. This is what we refer to as 'uni-Americanism' presented as multilateralism, and a facade that violates the whole principle of multilateralism. The system of multilateral institutions and the associated practice of multilateralism was established on the basis of a hegemonic world order. None the less, this world order was not simply built on hegemonic domination, but on generalised principles of conduct. The acceptance of this has been the 'constitution' of the system of multilateral institutions, and it is precisely this constitution that a unilateral United States may undermine. With all their faults, the World Bank and other multilateral institutions are a potential bulwark against a world order dominated by the unilateral actions of a single powerful country – whether that country be the United States or any other. We believe there is a need for substantive reform in these institutions, but they should not be closed down. Recent popular protests against the 'three sisters' (the WTO, the IMF and the World Bank) are welcome if they encourage people to take an interest, and increase their knowledge. Informed criticism of the multilateral institutions is what is needed, not the adoption of simplistic positions either in favour of, or in opposition to them. We hope that this book may make some contribution to such critical engagement, on a lasting basis, to ensure that these institutions serve the interests of both the rich and poor of the world.

Notes

CHAPTER 1

1. By inside/outside we are here referring to R.B.J. Walker's critique of traditional international relations theory (see Walker 1993).

CHAPTER 2

1. Source: (World Bank, 17 September 2001), see <http://www.worldbank.org/about/organisation/voting/lida.htm>
2. The only main exception to this picture is the AfDB whose rating in 1995 was reduced to double-A by the major credit-rating agencies. According to Standard & Poor's Sovereign Reports (1996), the main reason for this was the politicisation of the AfDB's corporate governance and management structure, a development that weakened its financial flexibility and set the AfDB apart from other multilateral development institutions in Standard & Poor's highest rating category.
3. In the late 1980s, the Asian Development Bank served as the testing ground for Japan's challenge to the US; in the 1990s it was the World Bank. Several of the arguments used by Japan in the ADB later spilled over to the debate in the World Bank about Japan's call for a study of economic growth in East Asia. For further details see Yasutomo (1995).
4. Source: IMF (2002b), <http://www.imf.org/external/np/sec/memdir/eds.htm>.
5. The US in the 1980s, for example, was an exception. It was able to run a huge deficit for a substantial period, since countries were quite willing to hold dollars.
6. The wake-up call for the US was the very hostile reception of Vice-President Richard Nixon during his May 1958 tour.
7. Prior to 1994, this board was called the Governing Council.
8. See *Rules of Procedure of the Executive Board of the United Nations Development Programme and the United Nations Population Fund.*
9. The proportion of UNDP core resources in comparision to non-core resources (for example, trust funds, cost-sharing, etc.) fell from 98 per cent in the period 1973–75 to 51 per cent in 1995, and to approximately 40 per cent in 2002 (see Klingebiel 1999 and UNDP 2002).
10. See, for example, *African Business*, January 2002.
11. The only important exception is the European Bank for Reconstruction and Development. This MDB was established after the end of the Cold War with the explicit objective of transforming the former planned economies of Eastern Europe into market economies.
12. See, for instance, the statements made by the Argentine government in response to the IMF's verdict on Argentina's financial crisis in August 2001 (*Financial Times*, 9 August 2001: 8).

13. The AfDB used to be in the forefront of regional development bank opposition to the World Bank; however, in the aftermath of the political and financial crisis that the AfDB experienced in the period from 1994 to 1996, this institution has at least rhetorically accepted the supremacy of World Bank approaches and policies in exchange for new funding for its soft-window facility, the African Development Fund.

CHAPTER 3

1. The UNDP is not explicitly included in this chapter. This is because it is taken up in Chapter 4, which analyses the developments within UNDP regarding 'governance' as an interesting manifestation of inter-institutional competition (in this case with the World Bank).
2. The first IDA credit was given to Honduras in 1961.
3. It is interesting to note the kind of similarity that exists between Bauer's argument and the post-development critique of the 1990s. See for instance, Escobar (1995).
4. Here the 1976 International Labour Organisation (ILO) Conference and the role of the United States is an interesting reference point.
5. It was proposed in 1967 by George Woods, president of the World Bank, and set up by his successor, Robert McNamara, in 1968.
6. The history of the past two decades has many examples of the efforts of the developing countries to create institutions in which they would have a decisive voice, but all such efforts have demonstrated the difficulty which such institutions experience in raising funds for their activities. A case in point is that of the UN Capital Development Fund which came into existence in 1966 after almost two decades of vigorous opposition and has received no contribution from the industrialised countries.
7. The Pearson and Brandt Reports are important and interesting milestones in the mapping of the international (Western) consensus. Both were set up at the initiative of the World Bank.
8. We will later consider the part played by the Pelosi Amendment in changing the environmental policies and procedures of multilateral institutions.
9. The establishment of SAPs also had several important implications for the relationship between the World Bank and the IMF. This is an issue we will return to at the end of this chapter when we consider policy changes across the spectrum of multilateral institutions.
10. Those particularly interested should consult Mosley et al. (1994), Mohan et al. (2000), the results from the ten-year research programme 'The Political and Social Context of Structural Adjustment in Sub-Saharan Africa' carried out at the Nordic Africa Institute (see <http://www.nai.uu.se/forsk/avslut/sap/sapsve.html>) and the NGO review of structural adjustment (see <http://www.saprin.org>).
11. The idea was that these institutions would provide for much higher levels of capital transfer than would otherwise be the case.
12. The information concerning this case was obtained from interviews with former and present AfDB staff, from Shaw (1991) and from two internal AfDB memoranda (AfDB 1987a and 1987b).

13. This film was made by a South African and in Botswana it was rumoured that the production of the film was sponsored by the South African meat industry in order to create trouble for the similar industry in Botswana (see Bøås 2001a).

14. The only references to the environment in GATT rules are GATT Article XX: general exception; (b) 'necessary to protect human, animal or plant life or health' and (g) 'relating to the conservation of exhaustible natural resources if such measures are made effectively in conjunction with restrictions on domestic production or consumption' (see GATT 1992).

15. The agenda for the Uruguay Round was agreed upon in Punta del Este, Uruguay in December 1986. The report of the WCED was launched four months later. In the report of the WCED both development and environmental preservation are emphasised and the report tries to strike a balance between them. The concept of sustainable development was not new, but the WCED gave it a new and broader definition than the former more narrow environmental interpretation of the concept. The WCED underscored *solidarity* both within and between generations by defining sustainable development as that which 'meet(s) the needs of the present without compromising the ability of future generations to meet their own' (WCED 1987: 43).

16. See United States Public Law 92–5222, 86, Stat. 1027.

17. Another reason for the lack of opposition to the revival of EMIT may be that principle 12 of the Rio Declaration ascertained that 'states should co-operate to promote a supportive and open international economic system that would lead to economic growth and sustainable development' (Petersmann 1995). In other words, in the Rio Declaration, trade liberalisation and sustainable development were seen as complementary, meaning that the trade–environment nexus was defined in a way which at least made possible its inclusion in the dominant perspective in GATT.

18. For a more comprehensive account of the dispute settlement mechanism see Bøås and Vevatne (2003).

19. The background for the shrimp–turtle dispute is that in 1997, India, Malaysia, Pakistan and Thailand sent a letter of complaint to the WTO stating that section 609 of the US Environmental Species Act violates the WTO's care rules concerning non-discrimination. Section 609 demanded that shrimp could only be imported into the US if it was clearly documented that the shrimping nets were equipped with so-called 'turtle excluding devices (TEDs). The US shrimp fleet is equipped with TEDs, while the majority of South and Southeast Asian shrimp boats are not.

20. The relationship between some NGOs and important member states (the US in particular) of multilateral institutions is an issue we will return to in detail in Chapter 4.

21. It is noteworthy that this characterisation of Doha was not made by a radical NGO, but by *African Business*, a moderate business journal. Its correspondents were outraged with what they saw and heard at the Doha meeting.

22. For further information about so-called 'mission creep' debate, see McQuillan and Montgomery (1999).

23. Traditionally, the IMF's main focus was on encouraging state administrations to 'correct' macroeconomic imbalances, reduce inflation and embark on reforms amenable to the private sector and international capital. This may be called 'first-stage restructuring'.

CHAPTER 4

1. Originally both the local assembly and the mayor resisted the project. However, in 1992, the mayor changed his position, and in April 1993, the city assembly approved plans to start construction. This change in position from the mayor and the local assembly led to rumours about threats and bribery.
2. This section draws on Bøås (2001a and 2001b).
3. This typology was originally developed for analysing the negotiating behaviour of states in international environmental negotiations.
4. See U.S. Public Law 99–500. 99th Congress, 2nd session, 18 October 1986.
5. See U.S. Public Law 99–461. 99th Congress, 1st session, 19 December 1985.
6. See U.S. Public Law 100–461. 100th Congress, 2nd session, 1 October 1988.
7. See U.S. Public Law 101–240. 101st Congress, 1st session, 19 December 1989.
8. This claim is made not only in the traditional problem-solving literature such as Keohane (1984 and 1989) or Grieco (1990), but also in an astonishingly large part of the so-called critical international political economy literature; see for instance Gill (1990).
9. This section draws upon material ciriculated and published by INHURD International (1994), *Financial Times* (9 June 1994 and 22 October 1994), Friends of the Earth Japan (1997), Bøås (2001a) and interviews with NGO activists conducted at the ADB's 30th Annual Meeting in Fukuoka, Japan in May 1997. Representatives from INHURD International were supposed to have been present at this meeting, but they were denied accreditation by the Nepalese government.
10. The Environmental Defence Fund and Environmental Defence are different entities.
11. The source of the estimate for the number of migrant workers is unknown. The figures used by the NGOs were challenged by the ADB and the World Bank, but in vain. The multilateral institutions were in fact largely unable to get their version of the story across to the media.
12. For more information about the reaction from the Government of Nepal see Reuters Press Release, Kathmandu (4 August 1995).
13. In the Inter-American Development Bank this function is called the 'Independent Investigation Mechanism'. In 1996, the IDB received its first request for an independent investigation of alleged violations of IDB policies and procedures in the design and implementation of the Yacyreta Hydroelectric Project. This request was filed by a Paraguayan NGO, with both the World Bank Inspection Panel and the IDB's Investigation Mechanism. For further details see IDB (1997).

14. The possible extension of inspection policies to also include private sector loans and operations is currently under review in several multilateral institutions, including the World Bank and the ADB.
15. The existence of inspection functions is not widely advertised by multilateral institutions, and even in the cases when local groups are aware of their existence, the often impenetrable language of multilateral institutions may discourage them from even attempting to use these mechanisms.
16. The recent report from the International Commission on Large Dams (ICOLD) has surprised many by its relatively negative assessment of the merits of large dams. See ICOLD (2001).
17. The discussion from this workshop was distilled in a book written by Hilton Root *Small Countries – Big Lessons: Governance and the Rise of East Asia* (1996). This book is a serious attempt to formulate an Asian approach to governance. The main argument is that the uniqueness of East Asia lies in its capacity to implement successful economic and social policies. This contributed to the later definition of good governance as sound development management.
18. Richard Ponzio, quoted in Dam (2002).
19. Most of the information in this section is either from material produced by the NGO Forum on ADB or obtained from Morten Bøås' participation at the annual meetings of the ADB in 2000, 2001 and 2002.
20. It is still unclear why the project site was changed and when, but rumours, so far not substantiated, are in circulation about corruption related to expropriation of land. The authors would like to make it clear that the source of these rumours is not the NGO Forum on ADB or local activists from Klong Dan.
21. This is based on the assessment of Morten Bøås, who has followed this case closely.
22. The local activists from Klong Dan were present at both the Annual Meetings in 2001 and 2002. These meetings were held respectively in Honolulu and Shanghai.
23. These claims were supported by several findings from studies from Greenpeace Southeast Asia Toxic Campaign. The results from these studies indicated that even an advanced country like Australia had huge problems getting advanced wastewater plants like the one planned for Samut Prakarn to work as they were intended. See Greenpeace (2002).
24. This sequence draws upon ADB (2001) and ADB (2002b) and meetings Morten Bøås took part in at the ADB Annual Meeting in 2002 in Shanghai, China.
25. It is interesting to note that the three major regional donor countries – Japan, Australia and New Zealand – did not take an active part in the discussion about Samut Prakarn.
26. In terms of the analysis of Pieterse (2001), 'development', to which 'post-development' is a reaction, implies an authoritarian and engineering approach, and spells disaster for local populations; while 'development' in the latter approach implies growth, and political and social modernisation.
27. For comprehensive accounts of the World Bank's involvement in the Narmada project see Udall (2000) and Wade (2003).

28. Three of the EDs which were calling for a suspension represented the World Bank's largest shareholders – the United States, Germany and Japan. There is more to power in multilateral institutions than voting strength alone.

29. This decision was proposed by Democratic Representative Frank and supported by the chairmen of the appropriations subcommittees, Representative Obey (Democrat) and Senator Leahy (Republican). In 1994, just before the official celebration of the fiftieth anniversary of the Bretton Woods institutions, the US Congress announced comparable sanctions. Unless drastic reforms were implemented, the 1995 contribution would be cut by 50 per cent.

30. The outcome of the debate was a limited budget cut. See Chatterjee and Finger (1994).

31. The first proponent of this 'radical' solution was Patricia Adams from the Canadian NGO Probe Internations. See Adams (1991).

32. The leading NGOs behind this campaign were the Environmental Defense Fund, Development GAP, Friends of the Earth (United States) and Greenpeace (United States).

33. This happened in the Sardar Sarovar case in India. See Kroksnes (1997) and Friends of the Earth Japan (1997).

34. This campaign cost the World Bank between US$100,000 and US$200,000.

35. The ADB's 2001 annual meeting was originally supposed to have taken place in Seattle, but after the November 1999 events it was decided to move it to a more suitable location (that is, one easy to monitor and expensive to reach). This was Honolulu, which actively marketed itself as a 'safe haven' for international meetings. An example of a relatively minor event attracting attention is the World Bank's Annual Bank Conference of Development Economics (Europe). In 2002, this conference was originally supposed to take place in Sweden, but after the event in Gothenburg in June 2001, the Swedish government decided it had had enough of such meetings for quite some time. The meeting was therefore moved to Oslo, Norway. Immediately, local groups established an umbrella organisation called Oslo 2002 in order to use this event to protest against the World Bank.

36. The argument for closure has also been directed towards the ADB and IDB.

CHAPTER 5

1. There are some who see these institutions as an embodiment of the 'institutionalisation' of the global reach of the market economy, and argue the case for closure of the World Bank and other multilateral institutions as part of a broader revolutionary struggle.

2. As an example see Cutler, Haufler and Porter (1999a: 16): 'Private firms and industry associations displayed an unprecedented prominence in the Uruguay Round of trade negotiations, the conclusion of the North American Free Trade Agreement, and negotiations over a variety of issues within the European Union. They were highly visible in the negotiations

leading up to the United Nations Conference on the Environment and Development in Rio De Janeiro, and have become integrated into decision-making processes with regard to the Montreal Protocol on Ozone abatement. Even in national security issue areas we see the participation of firms in lobbying, decision-making, and implementation in the Chemical Weapons Treaty. Major firms often now have official positions both within the domestic political structure, such as through industry advisory panels, and also within the international institutions where negotiations take place.'

3. These principles are: (1) support and respect for the protection of internationally proclaimed human rights; (2) noncomplicity in human rights abuses; (3) freedom of association and the effective recognition of the right to collective bargaining; (4) the elimination of all forms of forced and compulsory labour; (5) the effective abolition of child labour; (6) the elimination of discrimination in respect of employment and occupation; (7) a precautionary approach to environmental challenges; (8) greater environmental responsibility, and (9) encouragement of the development and diffusion of environmentally friendly technologies.

4. For example, the ILO has worked with employers' organisations for many years.

5. Rockefeller and Ford have been involved with multilateral institutions since the 1950s when agronomists at Rockefeller persuaded the World Bank to help Rockefeller and Ford to launch the 'Green Revolution'. The World Bank made credit available to farmers for advanced machinery, farm chemicals, seeds and livestock, but credit approval was conditional on farmers adopting new techniques, switching to particular crops and selling to a specific buyer who deducted the loan payments from the farmer's earnings. Yield per acre was the yardstick of social progress, and yield per capita of national stability; and in the context of the Cold War, stability was seen as the antidote to insurgency. The Green Revolution has therefore been regarded by some as a techno-functional fix to prevent communist revolutions; and technical progress as a viable alternative to land reform (see Dowie 2001 for further details).

6. Although this is the formal model of multilateral institutions, it is a huge simplification. Multilateral institutions have never operated only in accordance with formal rules. See Cox and Jacobsen (1977) and Bøås (2001a).

7. For instance, the World Bank initiated the Global Development Network and the associated Global Knowledge Network.

8. In fact, one of the main external achievement of ASEAN is its success in coordinating joint ASEAN positions on issues such as the trade–environment debate in the WTO (see Bøås 2000). On the issue of Japanese public opinion on ODA see Bøås (2002).

9. For instance, the Reagan administration used the Gonzalez Amendment, which states that the US cannot approve of loans to countries which have unfairly expropriated the property of American citizens or companies, to oppose MDB loans to Ethiopia. This was simply a way of justifying opposition to loans to a Marxist regime.

10. For a critique of the ADB approach to the Mekong see Öjendal (2000: 13) who argues that the ADB has initiated a huge neo-functional

development scheme 'which is potentially rivaling with the Mekong River Commission for initiative and attention.'

11. These are Puebla, Veracruz, Oaxaca, Chiapas, Tabasco, Campeche, Yucatàn and Quintana Roo.

12. The intended purpose of the scheme is to compete with the Southeast Asian assembly industry. Critics claim that in this process 'Meso-America' will be turned into the 'poor-man's region', in service of the rich North, and thus will move the boundary between rich and poor southwards and cut Mexico in two. More information about the resistance to the Plan Puebla Panama can be obtained from the Bank Information Center, a Washington DC-based NGO which coordinates NGO efforts to stop the plan. See <http://www.bicusa.org/>

13. Examples of this literature include Keohane (1984) and Kennedy (1988).

14. For instance Cox (2002: 68) argues that 'it is always wise to talk to one's friends. This is one of the lessons – amongst others – that US policy-makers seem to have learned from the tragedy visited upon the American republic on that bright and deadly morning in late 2001.' But multi-lateralism means more than just talking to one's friends.

Internet Resources

MULTILATERAL INSTITUTIONS

Abbr.	Institution	URL-Address
AfDB	African Development Bank	http://www.afdb.org
ADB	Asian Development Bank	http://www.adb.org
IDB	Inter-American Development Bank	http://www.iadb.org
IMF	International Monetary Fund	http://www.imf.org
UNDP	United Nations Development Programme	http://www.undp.org
WB	World Bank	http://www.worldbank.org
WTO	World Trade Organisation	http://www.wto.org

INTERNATIONAL ADVOCACY NGOS (SELECTED)

Abbr.	Institution	URL-Address
ATTAC	ATTAC (International portal)	http://www.attac.org
BIC	Bank Information Center	http://www.bicusa.org
BWP	Bretton Woods Project	http://www.brettonwoodsproject.org
CNES	Citizens' Network On Essential Services	http://www.servicesforall.org (formerly Globalization Challenge Initiative)
EURODAD	European Network on Debt and Development	http://www.eurodad.org
——	Focus on the Global South	http://www.focusweb.org
FOEI	Friends of the Earth International – Civil Society Control over IFIs	http://www.foei.org/ifi/civil.html
——	Jubilee South	http://www.jubileesouth.org
MGJ	Mobilization for Global Justice	http://www.globalizethis.org/fightback
SAPRIN	Structural Adjustment Participatory Review International Network	http://www.saprin.org
TWN	Third World Network	http://www.twnside.org.sg
——	WTO Watch	http://www.tradeobservatory.org
FoE	Friends of the Earth, US	http://www.foe.org/international/imf

168

FoE	Friends of the Earth, US	http://www.foe.org/ international/worldbank
——	Environmental Defence	http://www. environmentaldefense.org
——	Earth Island Institute	http://www.earthisland.org/ggn
WWF	World Wildlife Fund	http://www.panda.org/ resources/programmes/mpo
	International	http://www.panda.org/ resources/programmes/trade

REGIONAL ADVOCACY NGOS (SELECTED)

Region	Institution	URL-Address
Europe	CEE Bankwatch Network (Central and Eastern Europe)	http://www.bankwatch.org
Asia	NGO Forum on ADB Mekong Watch, Japan Greenpeace Southeast Asia	http://www.forum-adb.org http://www.mekongwatch.org http://www. greenpeacesoutheastasia.org
Africa	Uganda Debt Network Southern and Eastern Africa Trade Information And Negotiations Initiative	http://www.udn.or.ug http://www.seatini.org
Latin America	RedBancos, Latin American	http://fp.chasque.apc.org: 8081/redbancos
	Network on IFIs Trasparencia, Mexico	http://www.trasparencia.org.mx
	Instituto del Tercer Mundo, Uruguay	http://www.item.org.uy
	Red Mexicana de Acción al Frente al Libre Commercio	http://www.rmalc.org.mx
	Centro de Estudios Internacionales, Nicaragua	http://www.ceinicaragua.org.ni

Bibliography

Abrahamsen, R. (2000) *Disciplining Democracy: Development Discourse and Good Governance in Africa* (London: Zed Books).

Acharya, A. (1998) 'Collective Identity and Conflict Management in Southeast Asia', in E. Adler and M. Barnett (eds) *Security Communities* (Cambridge: Cambridge University Press), pp. 198–227.

Adams, P. (1991) *Odious Debts: Loose Lending, Corruption, and the Third World's Environmental Legacy* (London: Earthscan).

ADB (1966) *Agreement Establishing the Asian Development Bank* (Manila: ADB).

ADB (1995) *Governance: Sound Development Management* (Manila: ADB).

ADB (2001) *Final Report of Inspection Panel on Samut Prakarn Wastewater Management Project* (Manila: ADB).

ADB (2002a) *Annual Report 2001* (Manila: ADB).

ADB (2002b) *Samut Prakarn Wastewater Management Project Inspection: Management Response to the Final Report of the Inspection Panel* (Manila: ADB).

AfDB (1964) *Agreement Establishing the African Development Bank* (Abidjan: AfDB).

AfDB (1987a) *Memorandum: Botswana – Loan Proposal for the Financing of the Francistown Abattoir Project* (Abidjan: AfDB).

AfDB (1987b) *Memorandum: Botswana – Francistown Abattoir Project; Answers to Questions Raised by Directors* (Abidjan: AfDB).

AfDB (1996) *Annual Report 1995* (Abidjan: AfDB).

AfDB (2002) *Annual Report 2001* (Abidjan: AfDB).

African Business (January 1994).

African Business (January 2002).

Aufderheide, P. and B. Rich (1988) 'Environmental Reforms and the Multilateral Development Banks', *World Policy Journal*, vol. 5, pp. 301–21.

Bauer, P.T. (1972) *Dissent on Development: Studies and Debates in Development Economics* (Cambridge, MA: Harvard University Press).

Bergesen, H. and L. Lunde (1999) *Dinosaurs or Dynamos? The United Nations and The World Bank at the Turn of the Century* (London: Earthscan Publications Ltd).

Bøås, M. (2000) 'The Trade-Environment Nexus and the Potential of Regional Trade Institutions', *New Political Economy*, vol. 5, no. 3, pp. 415–32.

Bøås, M. (2001a) *Governance, Leadership and Ownership: The Case of the African Development Bank and the Asian Development Bank 1979–1996* (Oslo: Department of Political Science, Faculty of Social Sciences, University of Oslo), PhD Thesis.

Bøås, M. (2001b) 'Multilateral Development Banks, Environmental Impact Assessments, and Nongovernmental Organizations in U.S. Foreign Policy', in P.G. Harris (ed.) *The Environment, International Relations, and U.S. Foreign Policy* (Washington, DC: Georgetown University Press), pp. 178–96.

Bøås, M. (2002) *Public Attitudes to Aid in Norway and Japan* (Oslo: Centre for Development and the Environment, University of Oslo), Working Paper 2002: 3.

Bøås, M. and D. McNeill (eds) (2003) *Global Institutions and Development: Framing the World?* (London: Routledge), forthcoming.

Bøås, M. and J. Vevatne (2003) 'Sustainable Development and the World Trade Organisation', in M. Bøås and D. McNeill (eds) *Global Institutions and Development: Framing the World?* (London: Routledge), forthcoming.

Braathen, E. (2000) 'New Social Corporatism: a Discursive-Critical Review of the WDR 2000/1 Attacking Poverty', *Forum for Development Studies*, vol. 27, no. 2, pp. 331–50.

Brandt, W. (1980) *North–South: A Programme for Survival – a Report of the Independent Commission on International Development Issues* (Cambridge, MA: The MIT Press).

Bull, B. (2002) *Aid, Power, and Privatization: Domestic and International Sources of Telecommunication Reform in Central America (1986–2000)* (Oslo: Centre for Development and the Environment, University of Oslo), PhD Thesis.

Bull, B. and M. Bøås (2003) 'Regional Development Banks as Regionalising Actors: The Case of the Asian Development Bank and the Inter-American Development Bank', *New Political Economy* (forthcoming).

Burnham, P. (2001) 'New Labour and the Politics of Depoliticisation', *British Journal of Politics and International Relations*, vol. 3, no. 2, pp. 127–49.

Buzan, B., J. de Wilde and O. Wæver (1998) *Security: A New Framework for Analysis* (Boulder, CO: Lynne Rienner).

Camdessus, M. (1998) 'The IMF and Good Governance', Address by Managing Director of the International Monetary Fund at Transparency International (France), Paris, 21 January 1998, <http://www.imf.org/external/np/speeches/1998/012198.htm>.

Caufield, C. (1996) *Masters of Illusion: The World Bank and the Poverty of Nations* (New York: Henry Holt and Company).

Chatterjee, P. and M. Finger (1994) *The Earth Brokers: Power, Politics and World Development* (London: Routledge).

Chenery, H. (1974) 'Introduction', in H. Chenery, M.S. Ahluwalia, C.L.G. Bell, J.H. Duloy and R. Jolly (eds) *Redistribution with Growth* (Oxford: Oxford University Press), pp. vi–xvii.

Chenery, H. and A.M. Strout (1966) 'Foreign Assistance and Economic Development', *American Economic Review*, vol. 56, no. 4, pp. 391–416.

Chino, T. (2002) *Address to the Board of Governors: Strengthening Partnerships for Poverty Reduction in Asia and the Pacific* (Shanghai: ADB).

Cox, M. (2002) 'September 11th and U.S. Hegemony – Or Will the 21st Century be American Too?', *International Studies Perspectives*, vol. 3, no. 1, pp. 53–70.

Cox, R. (1992) 'Multilateralism and World Order', *Review of International Studies*, vol. 18, no. 2, pp. 161–80.

Cox, R.W. (1981) 'Social Forces, Stats, and World Orders', *Millennium*, vol. 10, no. 2, pp. 162–75.

Cox, R.W. (ed.) (1997) *The New Realism: Perspectives on Multilateralism and World Order* (New York: Macmillan and United Nations University Press).

Cox, R.W. and H.K. Jacobson (1977) 'Decision Making', *International Social Science Journal*, vol. 29, no. 1, pp. 115–35.

Culpeper, R. (1997) *Titans or Behemonths?* (Boulder, CO: Lynne Rienner).

Cutler, A.C., V. Haufler, and T. Porter (1999a) 'Private Authority and International Affairs', in A.C. Cutler, V. Haufler, and T. Porter (eds) *Private Authority and International Affairs* (New York: State University of New York Press), pp. 3–28.

Cutler, A.C, V. Haufler, and T. Porter (1999b) 'The Contours and Significance of Private Authority', in A.C. Cutler, V. Haufler, and T. Porter (eds) *Private Authority and International Affairs* (New York: State University of New York Press), pp. 333–76.

Dam, T. (2002) *Ideas and Institutions in the Multilateral Development System – an Analysis of UNDP's Adoption of the Idea of Good Governance* (Oslo: Centre for Development and the Environment), MA Thesis.

Dowie, M. (2001) *American Foundations – An Investigative History* (Cambridge, MA: The MIT Press).

Downs, A. (1957) *An Economic Theory of Democracy* (New York: Harper & Row).

Edgren, G. and B. Möller (1991) 'The Agencies at a Crossroad: The Role of the United Nations Specialized Agencies', in U. Rundin (ed.) *The United Nations: Issues and Options – Five Studies on the Role of the UN in the Economic and Social Fields* (Stockholm: Almqvist & Wiksell), pp. 115–78.

Emmerij, L., R. Jolly and T.G. Weiss (2001) *Ahead of the Curve? UN Ideas and Global Challenges* (Bloomington: Indiana University Press).

Escobar, A. (1995) *Encountering Development: The Making and Unmaking of the Third World* (Princeton, NJ: Princeton University Press).

Esty, D. (1994) *Greening the GATT: Trade, Environment, and the Future* (Washington, DC: Institute for International Economics).

Far Eastern Economic Review (20 March 1993).

Fidler, S. (2001) 'Who's Minding the Bank?', *Foreign Policy*, September/October, pp. 1–8.

Financial Times (9 June 1994).

Financial Times (22 October 1994).

Financial Times (9 August 2001).

Financial Times (10 May 2002).

Fitzpatrick, M. (1999) 'Protesters Claim WTO Failure as Victory', <http://biz.yahoo.com/rf/991204/bj.html>.

Focus on the Global South (2002) *Good Governance or Bad Management: An Overview of the ADB's Decision Making Process and Policies* (Bangkok: Focus on the Global South).

Fox, J.A. and L.D. Brown (2000a) 'Introduction', in J.A. Fox and L.D. Brown (eds) *The Struggle for Accountability: The World Bank, NGOs, and Grassroots Movements* (Cambridge, MA: The MIT Press), pp. 1–47.

Fox, J.A. and L.D. Brown (2000b) 'Assessing the Impact of NGO Advocacy Campaigns on World Bank Projects and Policies', in J.A. Fox and L.D. Brown (eds) *The Struggle for Accountability: The World Bank, NGOs, and Grassroots Movements* (Cambridge, MA: The MIT Press), pp. 485–551.

Friends of the Earth Japan (1997) *NGO Guide to Japan's ODA* (Japan: Yen Aid Watch Special Issue).

Gardner, K. and D. Lewis (1996) *Anthropology, Development and the Postmodern Challenge* (London: Pluto Press).

GATT (1972) *International Pollution Control and International Trade* (Geneva: GATT).

GATT (1992) *Trade and Environment Report* (Geneva: GATT).

George, S. and F. Sabelli (1994) *Faith and Credit: The World Bank's Secular Empire* (Harmondsworth: Penguin).

Gill, S. (1990) *American Hegemony and the Trilateral Commission* (Cambridge: Cambridge University Press).

Gill, S. (1998) 'New Constitutionalism, Democratisation and Global Political Economy', *Pacifica Review*, vol. 10, no. 1, pp. 23–38.

Greenpeace (2002) *Southeast Asia Toxics Campaign: Common Effluent Treatment Plants Don't Work* (Quezon City: Greenpeace).

Gricco, J. (1990) *Cooperation Among Nations* (Ithaca, NY: Cornell University Press).

Grindle, M. (2001) 'In Quest of the Political: The Political Economy of Development Policy-making', in G. Meier and J. Stiglitz (eds) *Frontiers in Development Economics: the Future In Perspective* (Oxford: Oxford University Press), pp. 62–76.

Guttal, S. (2002) 'A Master-plan for Market Expansion: The Asian Development Bank and Governance', in Focus on the Global South (ed.) *Good Governance or Bad Management: An Overview of the ADB's Decision Making Processes and Policies* (Bangkok: Focus on the Global South), pp. 3–6.

Gwin, C. (1994) *U.S. Relations with the World Bank 1945–92* (Washington, DC: The Brookings Institution).

Haas, E. (1990) *When Knowledge is Power – Three Models of Change in International Organizations* (Berkeley: University of California Press).

Haq, M. ul (1995) *Reflections on Human Development* (Oxford: Oxford University Press).

Harboe, H. (1989) *Economic Development and Environmental Concern: Modeling of Environmental Consequences in Development Projects* (Oslo: NUPI).

Herrera, F. (1974) *América Latina: Experiencias y Desafíos* (Buenos Aires: Instituto para la Integración de América Latina, IDB).

Hobsbawm, E. (1994) *Ages of Extremes: the Short Twentieth Century 1914–1991* (London: Michael Joseph).

ICOLD (2001) *Report From the Internatinal Commission on Large Dams* (Geneva: ICOLD).

IDB (1997) *Annual Report on the Environment and Natural Resources* (Washington, DC: IDB).

IDB (2002) *Annual Report 2001* (Washington, DC: IDB).

IDS (2000) *A Foresight and Policy Study of the Multilateral Development Banks* (Sussex: Institute of Development Studies, University of Sussex), prepared for the Ministry for Foreign Affairs, Sweden.

IMF (1997a) 'The Role of the IMF in Governance Issues: Guidance Note', <http://www.imf.org/external/pubs/ft/exrp/govern/govindex.htm>.

IMF (1997b) 'Good Governance: The IMF's Role', <http://imf.org/external/pubs/ft/exrp/govern/govindex.htm>.

IMF (2002a) *Annual Report 2001* (Washington, DC: IMF).

IMF (2002b) <http://www.imf.org/external/np/sec/memdir/eds.htm>.

INHURD International (1994) *Newsletter from the Arun Concerned Group* (Kathmandu: INHURD International).

Jerlström, B. (1990) *Banking on Africa: An Evaluation of the African Development Bank* (Stockholm: Ministry for Foreign Affairs).

Johnston, A.I. (2001) 'Treating International Institutions as Social Environments', *International Studies Quarterly*, vol. 45 no. 4, pp. 487–515.

Kalderén, L. (1991) 'The UN and the Bretton Woods Institutions', in U. Rundin (ed.) *The United Nations Issues and Options: Five Studies on the Role of the UN in the Economic and Social Fields Commissioned by the Nordic UN Project* (Stockholm: Almqvist & Wiksell International), pp. 323–56.

Kapur, D. and R. Webb (2000) *Governance-related Conditionalities of the International Financial Institutions* (New York and Cambridge, MA: G-24 Discussion Paper Series, no. 6, United Nations Conference on Trade and Development/Center for International Development, Harvard University).

Kennedy, P. (1988) *The Rise and Fall of the Great Powers: Economic Change and Military Conflict from 1500 to 2000* (New York: Random House).

Keohane, R. (1990) 'Multilateralism: An Agenda of Research', *International Journal*, vol. 45, no. 4, pp. 731–64.

Keohane, R.O. (1984) *After Hegemony* (Princeton, NJ: Princeton University Press).

Keohane, R.O. (1989) *International Institutions and State Power: Essays in International Relations Theory* (Boulder, CO: Westview Press).

Klingebiel, S. (1999) *Effectiveness and Reform of the United Nations Development Programme* (London: Frank Cass).

Kolk, A. (1996) *Forests in International Environmental Politics: International Organizations, NGOs and the Brazilian Amazon* (Utrecht: International Books).

Kratochwil, F. and J.G. Ruggie (1986) 'International Organization: a State of the Art or an Art of the State', *International Organization*, vol. 40, no. 4, pp. 753–75.

Krause, K. (2001) 'Constructing International Order: Multilateralism, the United Nations System and International Security', in P. Régnier and D. Wagner (eds) *Japan and Multilateral Diplomacy* (Aldershot: Ashgate), pp. 25–47.

Kroksnes, I. (1997) *Non-governmental Organizations and Development Policies: Identifying and Explaining Strategies – The Case of the World Bank's Narmada Dam Project* (Lysaker, Norway: The Fridtjof Nansen Institute).

Legum, C. (ed.) (1970) *The First U.N. Development Decade and its Lessons for the 1970s* (New York: Praeger).

Lund-Thomsen, P. (1999) *The Politics of Trade and Environment in the World Trade Organization* (Copenhagen: Copenhagen Business School, Department of Intercultural Management and Communication), MA Thesis.

Madrid Declaration of the Alternative Forum (1994) *50 Years is Enough* (Madrid: Alternative Forum).

McQuillian, L.J. and P.C. Montgomery (1999) *The International Monetary Fund: Financial Medic to the World?* (Stanford: Hoover Institution Press).

Mingst, K.A. (1990) *Politics and the African Development Bank* (Lexington: University of Kentucky Press).

Mohan, G., M. Brown, R. Milward and A. Zack-Williams (2000) *Structural Adjustment: Theory, Practice and Impacts* (London: Routledge).

Mosley, P., J. Harrigan and J. Toye (1994) *Aid and Power: The World Bank and Policy-Based Lending, Volume II* (London: Routledge).

Nelson, P. (2000) 'Whose Civil Society? Whose Governance? Decisionmaking and Practice in the New Agenda at the Inter-American Development Bank and the World Bank', *Global Governance*, vol. 6, no. 4, pp. 405–31.

NGO Forum on ADB (2002) *NGO Views on the Asian Development Bank: A Briefing Kit Prepared on the Occasion of the 35th ADB Annual Meeting* (Quezon City: NGO Forum on ADB).

Nordic Africa Institute (2002) <http://www.nai.uu.se/forsk/avslut/sapsve.html>.

Nördström, H. and S. Vaughan (1999) *Trade and Environment* (Geneva: WTO Special Studies No. 4).

Nustad, K.G. (2003) 'The Development Discourse in the Multilateral System', in M. Bøås and D. McNeill (eds) *Global Institutions and Development: Framing the World?* (London: Routledge), forthcoming.

Nustad, K.G. and O.J. Sending (2000) 'The Instrumentalisation of Development Knowledge', in D. Stone (ed.) *Banking on Knowledge: The Genesis of the Global Development Network* (London: Routledge), pp. 44–62.

O'Brien, R., A.M. Goetz, J.A. Scholte and M. Williams (2000) *Contesting Global Governance: Multilateral Economic Institutions and Global Social Movements* (Cambridge: Cambridge University Press).

Öjendal, J. (2000) *Sharing the Good: Modes of Managing Water Resources in the Lower Mekong River Basin* (Gothenburg: Department of Peace and Development Research, Gothenburg University).

Olson, M. (1965) *The Logic of Collective Action: Public Goods and the Theory of Groups* (Cambridge, MA: Harvard University Press).

Onuf, N. (1998) 'Constructivism: a User's Manual', in V. Kubalkova, N. Onuf and P. Kowert (eds) *International Relations in a Constructed World* (Armonk, NY: M.E. Sharpe), pp. 58–78.

Orr, R.M. (1990) *The Emergence of Japan's Foreign Aid Power* (New York: Columbia University Press).

Pearson, L. (1969) *Partners in Development: Report of the Commission on International Development* (New York: Praeger).

Petersmann, E.U. (1995) *International and European Trade and Environmental Law After the Uruguay Round* (London: Kluwer).

Pieterse, J. (2001) *Development Theory: Deconstructions/Reconstructions* (London: SAGE Publications).

Porter, D.J. (1995) 'Scenes from Childhood. The Homesickness of Development Discourses', in J. Crush (ed.) *Power of Development* (London: Routledge), pp. 63–89.

Porter, G. and J.W. Brown (1996) *Global Environmental Politics* (Boulder, CO: Westview Press).

Reuters Press Release, Kathmandu (4 August 1995).

Rich, B. (1985) 'The Multilateral Development Banks, Environmental Policy and the United States', *Ecology Law Quarterly*, vol. 12, no. 2, pp. 681–745.

Rich, B. (1993) *Statement Concerning FY 1994 Appropriations* (Washington, DC: House Subcommittee on Appropriations).

Root, H. (1996) *Small Countries, Big Lessons – Governance and the Rise of East Asia* (Hong Kong: Oxford University Press).

Ruggie, J.G. (1993) 'Multilateralism: the Anatomy of an Institution', in J.G. Ruggie (ed.) *Multilateralism Matters: The Theory and Practice of an Institutional Form* (New York: Columbia University Press), pp. 3–47.

Ruggie, J.G. (2001) 'global_governance.net: The Global Compact as Learning Network', *Global Governance*, vol. 7, no. 4, pp. 371–8.

Sachs, W. (ed.) (1995) *The Development Dictionary: A Guide to Knowledge as Power* (Johannesburg: Witwatersrand Univeristy Press).

Sanford, J.E. (1982) *U.S. Foreign Policy and Multilateral Development Banks* (Boulder, CO: Westview Press).

Sanger, D.E. (1999) 'Runaway Agency or U.S. Pawn', in L.J. McQuillian and P.C. Montgomery (eds) *The International Monetary Fund: Financial Medic to the World?* (Stanford, CA: Hoover Institution Press), pp. 22–3.

Santiso C. (2001a) 'Good Governance and Aid Effectiveness: The World Bank and Conditionality', *The Georgetown Public Policy Review*, vol 7, no.1, pp. 1–22.

Santiso, C. (2001b) 'International Co-operation for Democracy and Good Governance: Moving Towards a Second Generation?', *The European Journal of Development Research*, vol. 13, no. 1, pp. 154–80.

Scholte, J.A. (2000) *Globalization a Critical Introduction* (Basingstoke: Macmillan).

Schoultz, L. (1982) 'Politics, Economics and U.S. Participation in Multilateral Development Banks', *International Organization*, vol. 36, no. 3, pp. 537–74.

Shaw, C.L (1991) 'Par Inter Paribus: The Nature of Power in Co-operation – Lessons (for the United States) From the African Development Bank', *African Affairs*, vol. 90, pp. 537–58.

Standard & Poor's (1996) *Supranationals – A Special Edition from Sovereign Reports* (New York: McGraw-Hill).

Standard & Poor's (2001) *Sovereign Ratings Service: Supranational Special Edition 2001* (New York: McGraw-Hill).

Stein, R. and B. Johnson (1979) *Banking on the Biosphere? Environmental Practice and Procedures of Nine Multilateral Development Agencies* (Lexington: IIED).

Strange, S. (1982) 'Cave! Hic Dragones: a Critique of Regime Analysis', *International Organization*, vol. 36, no. 2, pp. 479–97.

Taylor, I. (2003) 'Hegemony, Neo-liberal "Good Goverance" and the International Monetary Fund: A Gramscian Perspective', in M. Bøås and D. McNeill (eds) *Global Institutions and Development: Framing the World?* (London: Routledge), forthcoming.

Thant, M., M. Tang and H. Kakazu (eds) (1994) *Growth Triangles in Asia: a New Approach to Regional Economic Co-operation* (Hong Kong: Oxford University Press).

Transnational Resource and Action Center (2000) *Tangled Up in Blue: Corporate Partnerships at the United Nations* (San Francisco: TRAC).

Tussie, D. (1995) *The Inter-American Development Bank* (London: Intermediate Technology Publications).

Udall, L. (2000) 'The World Bank and Public Accountability: Has Anything Changed?', in J.A. Fox and L. Brown (eds) *The Struggle for Accountability: The World Bank, NGOs, and Grassroots Movements* (Cambridge, MA: The MIT Press), pp. 391–436.

UN (2001) *Towards Global Partnerships: Co-operation between the United Nations and all Relevant Partners, in Particular in the Private Sector* (New York: UN).

UNDP (1995) *Annual Report of the Administrator 1994* (New York: UNDP).

UNDP (1997) *Rules of Proceudres of the Executive Board of the United Nations Development Programme and the United Nations Population Fund* (New York: UN).

UNDP (2000a) *Annual Report of the Administrator 1999* (New York: UNDP).

UNDP (2000b) *The Way Forward: The Administrator's Business Plan* (New York: UNDP).

UNDP (2002) *Annual Report 2002* (New York: UNDP).

United States Public Law 92–5222, 86, Stat. 1027.

United States Public Law 99–461. 99th Congress, 1st session, 19 December 1985.

United States Public Law 99–500. 99th Congress, 2nd session, 18 October 1986.

United States Public Law 100–461. 100th Congress, 2nd session, 1 October 1988.

United States Public Law 101–240. 101st Congress, 1st session, 19 December 1989.

Vevatne, J. (2000a) *WTO, NGOer og Seattle: En Analyse av Miljøbevegelsens Forsøk på å Øve Innflytelse overfor Verdens Handelsorganisasjon* (Oslo: Department of Political Science, University of Oslo), MA Thesis.

Vevatne, J. (2000b) 'Skilpadder og Tåregass – Miljøbevegelsen versus WTO', *Internasjonal Politikk*, vol. 58, no. 4, pp. 527–57.

Wade, R. (1994) 'Is The East Asian Miracle Right?' in A. Fishlow, C. Gwin, S. Haggard, D. Rodrik and R. Wade (eds) *Miracle or Design? Lessons from the East Asian Experience* (Washington, DC: Overseas Development Council), pp. 55–79.

Wade, R. (2001) 'Showdown at the World Bank', *New Left Review*, vol. 7 (January/February), pp. 124–37.

Wade R. (2003) 'The World Bank and the Environment', in M. Bøås and D. McNeill (eds) *Framing the World: The Role of Ideas in Multilateral Institutions* (London: Routledge), pp. 40–59.

Walker, R.B.J. (1993) *Inside/Outside: International Relations as Political Theory* (Cambridge: Cambridge University Press).

WCED (1987) *Our Common Future* (Oxford: Oxford University Press).

World Bank (1976) *Summary Proceedings of the 1976 Annual Meetings of the Board of Governors* (Washington, DC: World Bank).

World Bank (1989) *Articles of Agreement* (Washington, DC: World Bank).

World Bank (1991) *Managing Development: The Governance Dimension* (Washington, DC: World Bank).

World Bank (1992) *Governance and Development* (Washington, DC: World Bank).

World Bank (1993) *The East Asian Miracle: Economic Growth and Public Policy* (Washington, DC: World Bank).

World Bank (1994a) *Adjustment in Africa: Reforms, Results and the Road Ahead* (Washington, DC: The World Bank).

World Bank (1994b) *Governance: The World Bank Experience* (Washington, DC: World Bank).

World Bank (2000) *Reforming Public Institutions and Strengthening Governance* (Washington, DC: The World Bank).

World Bank (2001) <http//:www.worldbank.org/about/organization/voting/lida.htm>.

World Bank (2002) *Annual Report 2001* (Washington, DC: World Bank).

World Bank and UNDP (1989) *Africa's Adjustment in the 1980s* (Washington, DC: World Bank).

WTO (1994) *Trade and Environment Decision of 14 April 1994* (Geneva: WTO).

WTO (2002) *Annual Report 2002* (Geneva: WTO).

Yasutomo, D.T. (1995) *The New Multilateralism in Japan's Foreign Policy* (London: Macmillan Press).

Index